100
Great
Monologs

A versatile collection of monologs,
duologs and triologs for student actors

Rebecca Young

MERIWETHER PUBLISHING LTD.
Colorado Springs, Colorado

Meriwether Publishing Ltd., Publisher
PO Box 7710
Colorado Springs, CO 80933-7710

Executive editor: Arthur L. Zapel
Editorial assistant: Dianne Bundt
Cover design: Janice Melvin

Library of Congress Cataloging-in-Publication Data

Young, Rebecca, 1965-
    100 great monologs : a versatile collection of monologs, duologs and triologs for student actors / by Rebecca Young.
        p. cm.
    ISBN 13: 978-1-56608-104-7
    ISBN 10: 1-56608-104-1
    1. Monologues. 2. Acting.   I. Title. II. Title: One hundred great monologs.
    PN2080.Y65 2005
    812'.6--dc22

2004024947

2   3   4   06   07   08

Dedication

For my mom, who encouraged me all my life to write; my awesome girls, who are just as excited as I am; my sister and brothers, who unknowingly provided great material; my writer friends, who never gave up on me; and my husband, Frank, who supported this dream. I love you all.

Contents

Section III: Monologs — That's the Way I See It! 69

Introduction

100 Great Monologs offers a variety of subject material. It was created with two purposes in mind: 1) to provide an acting tool for young actors, and 2) to get students talking. The unique format of this book offers group and duo monologs through which different viewpoints can be seen, yet the actors still do not interact. These can be great tools for opening up subjects for discussion or debate. The standard single monologs included in this collection also touch on issues that students may feel the need to discuss. Whether used for an audition, a class assignment, or as a method to start a discussion, *100 Great Monologs* offers something for everyone.

Each monolog has been kept short so it is perfect for a classroom setting (when all twenty-five to thirty students have to perform for a grade) or for an audition when time is limited (usually two to three minutes maximum).

As a mother of three, substitute teacher, and drama director for middle and high school students, I know the subject material of these monologs to be honest and true to life. Yet, as a teacher, parent, or young actor, you won't be embarrassed by inappropriate language or situations. These monologs don't skirt important issues that teens face today, but each situation is handled in a way that allows the actor to be center stage — not the language.

With one hundred monologs to choose from, there's certain to be one that speaks to your heart and gives you an outlet to shine. Good luck! I hope the thrill of acting for you is just one monolog away.

SECTION I
TRIOLOGS

It's All in How You See It!

A single scene seen entirely differently!

1. Who's to Blame?

(2 girls/1 guy)

Katie's Version

KATIE: I should've taken her keys. I know I should have, but I wasn't exactly thinking clearly either! It's a miracle I made it home alive as bad off as I was. So how can everyone pin this on me? They look at me like I'm some kind of murderer! I didn't see anyone else taking Jenna's keys — or mine for that matter! What if I'd been in an accident? Who would they be blaming then?

Is it my fault that I was the last one who saw her? Plenty of other kids saw her staggering around the party. Why didn't they do something? Her parents think I'm the one to blame ... well, what about the rest of the party? Or better yet, what about Jenna? She's the one who drank and then wrapped herself around a tree! She's the one who drove when she could barely walk to her car! Why aren't they blaming her? Or themselves? They brought her up. They raised her. Not me!

All I did was head out at the same time, talk to her for a minute and then leave. Why am I all of a sudden her keeper? I didn't even know her all that well. Who am I to stop her from doing what she wants?

I mean, don't get me wrong, it's not like I don't feel bad about it. I do. She died after all, and that's horrible! But it's not *my* fault, and I'm tired of everyone trying to make me feel guilty! We all make mistakes. This was hers, not mine!

I heard her parents are talking about pressing charges against me. Can they do that? I didn't drive her into that

1   tree! I wasn't anywhere near that car. How is it my fault
2   that she can't drive after a couple of beers?! Why don't
3   they sue Chad?! He's the one who had the party! Or the
4   person who brought the beer in the first place? They'll
5   probably end up suing everybody. They just don't want
6   to blame their precious little daughter. Or themselves.
7   It's easier for everyone to point the finger at me ... but I
8   didn't do it ... it's not my fault.
9

10   *Jenna's Mom's Version*
11 **JENNA'S MOM:** I'm never going to see Jenna again. Never
12   going to see her go to prom, graduate, get married ... have
13   children. Never. It's so unfair that our one and only child
14   was taken from us so unexpectedly. Snatched from our
15   lives in the middle of the night ... a night so horrifying it still
16   haunts me. The police officer coming to our door, the look
17   on his face when he told us what had happened, seeing my
18   daughter's mangled body on that cold metal bed ...
19   something no parent should ever have to go through!
20   And that's what makes me the maddest! I didn't have
21   to go through it either! There were plenty of people that
22   could have stopped this tragedy from happening. Plenty of
23   her so-called friends that should've known better than to
24   let her drive after drinking! And what about the parents
25   that had an unchaperoned party in the first place?! What
26   were they thinking leaving a house full of teenagers?
27   Then there's that one girl ... Katie ... they say she talked
28   to Jenna right before — *right before* — she got in the car
29   and drove off! Why didn't she have the sense to take the
30   keys? To stop my daughter from getting behind the wheel?
31   Jenna's life was in her hands and she just carelessly threw
32   it away! How could she do that? How can she ... how can
33   I ... live with that? That my daughter's life could've been
34   saved?! She would still be with us — smiling, laughing,
35   sometimes driving me crazy ... but *still with us* — if just

1   *one* person had cared enough to stop her!
2   All they had to do ... all *she* had to do ... was call. I
3   would've been there in a heartbeat. No questions asked.
4   Haven't I always told Jenna that? Never, *ever* drive after
5   drinking. Or get in a car with someone who's been
6   drinking. No matter where you are or what time it is ...
7   it's never too late to call me ... I'll be there ...
8   It's never too late ...
9   Only now. Now it's too late.
10   Oh, Jenna, why didn't you call me?
11
12   *Chad's Version*
13 CHAD: I can't believe that Jenna is dead. It's all so sudden.
14   So unreal. You hear about stuff like this happening but
15   you never think it's gonna happen to someone you know.
16   My parents are freaking out, too. They say that they
17   could lose everything because of me. How was I to know
18   she'd drive drunk? Just because I had the party, why
19   does that make me responsible? I didn't force her to
20   come — or drink so many beers! Is it my fault she got
21   drunk? Besides, all the parties have kegs or spiked
22   punch. Everyone would've thought I was lame if I hadn't
23   gotten some alcohol snuck in.
24   How can Jenna's parents blame us for her accident?
25   Maybe she hit a slick spot on the road — it was raining
26   that night, wasn't it? Or maybe a deer darted out in front
27   of her ... who's to say it was the alcohol that made her
28   wrap her car around that tree?! She was probably talking
29   on her cell phone ... has anyone thought of that? The
30   thing was practically attached to her ear whenever she
31   drove! Why don't they sue the cell phone company?
32   It's just ridiculous that we're all going to have to suffer
33   because of Jenna ... I mean, don't get me wrong, I feel
34   horrible that she's dead. She was smart, pretty, funny —
35   very popular, really — but dead is dead and her parents

1   pulling all of us through the mud is not going to bring her
2   back. They're just trying to make us feel guilty when it
3   wasn't anyone's fault but Jenna's.
4   Well, I hope everyone had fun that night because that's
5   the last party I'll ever be able to throw!

2. Custody Battle
(2 girls/1 guy)

1	*Tiara's Version*
2	TIARA: Today I have to do the hardest thing a girl can ever
3	do in her life. I have to testify against my mother in court.
4	I have to tell the world all of our horrible family secrets,
5	and the worst part is my mom will be listening the whole
6	time, probably crying hysterically.
7	See, my dad wants to have full custody of my brother
8	and me, and we want to be with him, too. It's not that
9	we don't love our mother; we're just tired of living with
10	her. She screams at us all the time over stupid things
11	and she's always threatening to send us to live with Dad
12	anyway. You'd think she'd be happy to get rid of us since
13	we seem to make her so miserable, but she's fighting
14	tooth and nail to keep us now.
15	I think she needs some kind of help or something. She
16	has these really bad mood swings. One second we'll be
17	laughing and having a good time and the next minute she's
18	screaming at us, telling us how ungrateful we are! She's
19	always saying how much she gives up so that she can
20	afford to feed and clothe us. I know she's making sacrifices,
21	but I'm tired of hearing about them every second. We didn't
22	ask for her and Dad to get divorced.
23	Every chance she gets, she's bad-mouthing Dad.
24	Saying everything is his fault, he's the one who left, he's
25	the one who doesn't pay enough child support, he's the
26	one with the new wife. We always feel so in the middle
27	when we're with her. Like the only way she'll love us is if
28	we talk bad about our dad and take her side.

1   Mom thinks that Dad turned us against her. She says
2   we weren't like this before, not wanting to be with her.
3   Well, to be honest, we never had a choice. Our parents
4   lived together, where were we gonna go? Mom's been a
5   screaming maniac for years now. Since way before the
6   divorce. She can blame it all on Dad, but the truth is,
7   she's never been a good mother. We weren't surprised
8   when Dad finally left. We wanted to go with him.
9   Still, it's hard to hurt my mom this way. I know she
10   thinks she's done her best all these years. I used to think
11   so, too, until I saw the way other families lived. I'd visit
12   a friend's house and be surprised that no one was
13   screaming. It's amazing how used to it we all got.
14   I hope Mom will get the help she needs. Maybe without
15   us, she'll figure out why she's so angry inside. I know
16   deep down she loves us — she's just forgotten how to
17   show it. Maybe one day she'll understand that I had to do
18   this. Maybe one day she'll forgive me.
19
20   *Mother's Version*
21 MOTHER: I don't understand what the big deal is. You
22   discipline your kids nowadays and everyone wants to try
23   and take them from you. It's ridiculous! So I yell at my
24   kids sometimes. Big deal. Show me a parent that
25   doesn't. If they'd just listen to me and do what I ask, I
26   wouldn't have to yell. Come on, it's not like I beat them
27   or anything — I've hardly ever even spanked them. How
28   can anyone say I'm an unfit mother?
29   This is all just a way for my ex-husband to stop paying
30   child support. He figures if they live with him he won't
31   have to pay me a dime. I'm not stupid. I can see how he's
32   brainwashing them. And bribing them! Oh, they've got it
33   all at his house. He even put in a pool this past summer!
34   Now how many years did I beg for that? He's just trying
35   to make it so fun at his house that they won't want to live

1   with me. Well, maybe if he paid a little more for his kids,
2   I could afford things like a pool or a new big screen TV. I
3   can't compete with that stuff. I'm a waitress for crying
4   out loud!
5   I just wish he'd quit trying to steal my kids away from
6   me. They need their mother — *me* — not his new wife!
7   She is not and will not ever be their mother and he'd
8   better come to grips with that! I'm so sick of the kids
9   telling me how great she is. Why can't everyone see this
10   is all just a big act? A ploy to take my kids? Scott and
11   Dawn wouldn't have them two seconds before they'd be
12   begging me to take them back! I'm the one who knows
13   how to handle them. I know how to keep them in line.
14   And I can do it without buying them a pool!
15
16   *Father's Version*
17 FATHER: I always knew my ex-wife was a horrible mother to
18   our children. I knew it but there wasn't much I could do
19   about it. I tried to make things as normal for them as I
20   could. I did everything to keep her from going off. See,
21   she has this yelling problem. You get her started and she
22   can scream at you for half an hour nonstop! I tried to
23   teach the kids to walk on eggshells whenever she was in
24   a mood. But that got to be twenty-four/seven, and they're
25   kids! They're not going to be perfect!
26   I hated to leave them behind when I moved out, but I
27   didn't have a choice. I'm trying to fix that now. Surely the
28   courts will agree the children would be better off living
29   with me ... and my new wife, Dawn. She's so good with
30   them. She's patient and kind and actually likes just
31   hanging out with them. When they stay with us,
32   everything is always so ... peaceful. Something that none
33   of us are used to.
34   I hate that the kids have to go through this. Especially
35   Tiara since they've asked her to testify against her mom.

1   I know that's very hard for her. I just wish Joy would stop

2   being so selfish and let them be where they want to be ...

3   with me. She's just afraid to lose child support. She

4   doesn't care about those kids. Half the time she's out on

5   a date when it's her weekend to have them. I just wish

6   for once she'd think of someone other than herself and

7   do the right thing.

8   I hope she loses it in court — the way she does at

9   home — then they'll see what she's really like. Then

10   they'll know what we're all talking about.

3. Wake-Up Call
(1 girl/2 guys)

1   *Macy's Version*

2 MACY: My ex-boyfriend is so weird! Sometimes I wonder why

3   I even went out with him in the first place. I knew he was

4   still upset about us breaking up, but I never thought he'd

5   show up at my house in the middle of the night!

6   There I was, sound asleep when something banged

7   against my bedroom window. A rock! I don't know how

8   many times he'd thrown one before it actually hit the

9   glass loud enough to wake me. But this one about broke

10   the windowpane, it hit so hard!

11   Anyway, I pushed up the window and there's Ernie

12   standing in the middle of our lawn. "What are you

13   doing?" I asked as loud as I could without waking my

14   parents up.

15   You know what the moron did? He started yelling how

16   much he loved me and can't live without me. He was

17   staggering all over our lawn, obviously drunk or high or

18   something! Well, of course, my parents couldn't sleep

19   through all that racket!

20   I heard Dad pound down the steps and then the front

21   porch light was flipped on. The yard was flooded in light.

22   You'd think Ernie would've had enough sense at that

23   point to jump in his car and speed off. But no! Not Ernie!

24   He acted like he'd been spotlighted for a show or

25   something. He started yelling louder and then even

26   started singing a love song! Badly, I might add, since

27   Ernie couldn't hear a pitch if he had to. See, I told you

28   he was weird!

1   Anyway, I thought my dad would be all mad and stuff,

2   maybe chase him off with a broom or a baseball bat or

3   something great like that. Maybe even call the cops on the

4   idiot! But what does *my* dad do? He goes out — in his

5   pajamas, mind you — not to hit or run Ernie off. But to

6   talk to him! And as if that's not strange enough, the next

7   thing I know, Dad's got his arm around the guy, bringing

8   him inside! I swear I don't know who's weirder! Now Dad

9   tells me that I have to be nice to Ernie. Says he needs time

10   to heal and get used to us being broken up — whose side

11   is he on anyway?

12   ... I guess I will though ... be nice to him ... 'cause I

13   sure don't want any more late night serenading! If he

14   thought that would win me back — he was drunker than

15   I thought!

16

17   *Father's Version*

18 FATHER: That was some kind of wailing going on in my yard

19   last night! I thought one of Mr. Jenkins' cows had broken

20   the fence and was dying on my front lawn! What kind of

21   idiot shows up in the middle of the night to win back his

22   girlfriend? And all that racket he was making sure wasn't

23   making *me* fall in love with him!

24   By the time I got out there he was belting out some

25   kind of love song that I sure didn't recognize — I don't

26   know if *he* even knew the words!

27   There I was, in my pajamas, out on my lawn with a

28   lovesick teenage boy who was ready to burst into tears.

29   That would've at least stopped the singing, but I could tell

30   that if he did start sobbing he wasn't going to do that

31   quietly either. He'd be wailing loud enough to wake the

32   dead pets we had buried in the backyard! So I did the only

33   thing I could do — I brought the pitiful guy inside. I could

34   hardly send him on his way, because his breath about

35   knocked me over when he belted out a tune right in my

1   face! Obviously he'd been trying to drown his sorrows.
2   So I fixed a pot of really strong coffee and talked to the
3   poor guy about heartache. Partly to make him feel a little
4   better and partly so I could see just how psycho he was.
5   I sure didn't want my daughter in the news for some
6   crazed maniac ex-boyfriend running off with her or
7   something worse!
8   He'd always seemed like a pretty good guy, and I could
9   tell he hadn't totally gone off the deep end. He was
10 heartbroken, that much was clear. Lovesick over my
11 daughter who broke up with him — in a letter, no less! I
12 could sympathize with the poor guy! Hey, we've all been
13 there before, right? I wanted to make her march
14 downstairs and apologize to the pitiful red-eyed thing
15 before me, but I knew better than to take sides on this.
16 I'd talk to her later about breaking up the right way —
17 face to face. For now, I poured coffee while the young
18 man poured out his heart. It was the least I could do.
19
20   *Ernie's Version*
21 ERNIE: I can't believe Macy dumped me! In a note, no less!
22   How bad is that? We've been dating almost a year and I
23   get a "Dear John" letter? It didn't even really explain
24   why — and that crap about still being friends? Why do
25   girls think that makes things better? I don't want to be
26   her friend. I want to be her boyfriend!
27   That's why I had to see her. To clear things up. I knew
28   once we had a chance to talk — face to face — she'd
29   take me back!
30   I didn't realize it'd gotten so late. I hung out at Dave's
31   house a little longer than I thought. You know, getting my
32   courage up. Having a couple of his dad's beers.
33   I didn't mean to make such a scene — only she
34   wouldn't come out! Wouldn't talk to me! Wouldn't even
35   give me a chance!

1   I don't know why I started singing. I just wanted her
2   to come outside so I could see her. I figured we'd work
3   things out. When the porch light came on, I thought it
4   was her. I should've known she couldn't get downstairs
5   that fast. But with the bright light blinding me, I didn't
6   know it was her dad until we were practically face to face!
7   Then it was too late to run!

8   I thought he was gonna kill me! But you know what he
9   did? He put his arm around me and brought me inside,
10 fixed a pot of coffee, and we talked for hours! I felt a lot
11 better after that. I just wish I'd known before we broke
12 up that Macy's dad was so cool!

4. Cheap Labor
(3 girls)

1   *Kathleen's Version*

2   KATHLEEN: The people across the street need to be put in

3   jail! I'm not kidding! They've been running that slave

4   camp for years and nobody does anything about it. One

5   girl gets old enough to leave and they send another! How

6   can the state call that a foster home? It's nothing but a

7   free labor house for Mr. and Mrs. Shores.

8   Those girls do everything around there. Housecleaning,

9   laundry, yard work — they even make them wash the

10   cars and plant a full garden! They're really getting their

11   money's worth! Oh wait! I forgot. That's the best part!

12   For the Shores! Not only do they get all this *free* work

13   out of these poor girls, they get *paid* from the state for

14   housing them. Ha!

15   They never spend any money on them. I think one of

16   the girls even sews all of their clothes! Talk about

17   cheapskates! Why does the state keep giving them girl

18   after girl to use as they want? I think they've got about

19   six over there right now. Doesn't that send up some kind

20   of red flag? What kind of people want six foster kids? And

21   no boys either. They must know a boy would never put

22   up with being treated like that!

23   The girls hardly ever leave the house. Mrs. Shores says

24   she homeschools them all. Says they're really smart young

25   ladies. Yeah, right. I bet none of them could pass the first

26   test at school. They're always so busy. How could they

27   possibly have time for schoolwork? And Mrs. Shores

28   doesn't seem smart enough to teach herself anything,

1   much less six girls at three different grade levels! I bet
2   those girls are just counting the days until they get to
3   leave! Eighteen and they're out of that labor camp! Then
4   they can get out on their own and do what they want and
5   not what Mr. and Mrs. Shores tell them to do!
6
7   *Chassidy's Version*
8 CHASSIDY: So many of the foster homes I've been in have
9   been real dumps. Usually I have to share a room with
10   kids that don't want me there. My stuff either ends up
11   stolen or broken and I get blamed somehow. Either I
12   "lost" it, or I left it out and that's why "Johnny" stepped
13   on it ... blah, blah, blah. I know the only reason people
14   take me in is so that they can live off the money the state
15   pays them.
16   But not this place. This place is awesome! There are
17   five other girls who live here, which I thought would be
18   awful at first, but it's worked out great. We're like one big
19   family. I don't even mind sharing a room with two others
20   because the rooms are pretty big and no one ever bothers
21   my stuff. It's so different from what I'm used to. We have
22   rules about respect and privacy and it's totally working
23   out great.
24   Mr. and Mrs. Shores are really nice. We all have
25   chores, sure, but that's the only way a household this
26   size can run as smoothly as it does. And they work hard,
27   too. Mrs. Shores is always staying up late trying to get
28   things done and Mr. Shores works long hours at his job.
29   I'm not saying we never complain, because of course
30   we do, but when everyone does his or her part, it's a
31   pretty well-greased wheel around here. And they let us
32   pick one chore that we really like and one chore that
33   nobody likes (like cleaning the toilets, which of course I
34   got!). For my choice chore, I picked the garden. I love
35   planting, weeding, and keeping the garden looking great.

1   It's peaceful out there, too. It gives me a chance to think.
2   And fresh vegetables are the best! I'd never really had
3   any before I came here. Only cheap generic vegetables
4   out of a can. Fresh is so much better!
5   Us helping out saves the Shores money, which is really
6   good. I know raising six kids, even with the state money,
7   can be pretty hard. Mrs. Shores is always poring over the
8   bills and the budget. We live pretty tight, but a lot more
9   comfortably than I've ever lived before, I can tell you that!
10   In fact, I'd say right now I'm living in the lap of luxury! I
11   wish every girl had it so good!
12
13   *Shawna's Version*
14 SHAWNA: I came to this house almost four years ago. I was
15   scared to death. The last foster parent I had beat me. I
16   didn't think it would be any different here. I remember
17   that I didn't even give it a chance. Ran away the very first
18   night. Of course they found me and brought me back. I
19   thought Mr. and Mrs. Shores would fly off the handle.
20   Scream and yell all night and then send me back to the
21   agency. They didn't. Not even when I ran away the
22   second night.
23   It was like that for a while. Looking back I realize how
24   stubborn I was about giving them a chance. You can't
25   really blame me though; everyone in my life up until that
26   point had let me down. I really didn't think these people
27   who didn't even know me would be any different. But they
28   were. They were so patient and kind and eventually I
29   stopped trying to run away. I settled in, got used to them,
30   and they got used to me.
31   There were some stumbling blocks for sure. I was
32   pretty defiant about the chore thing at first. I figured they
33   were getting paid to have me, why should I have to help
34   out? But even that worked out, especially when I got the
35   chore of hanging out the laundry. See, Mrs. Shores had

1   this thing about fresh sheets blowing in the wind. I'd
2   take a basket out, stand in the breeze, and clip sweet-
3   smelling sheets while the sun baked the back of my
4   neck. I grew to really enjoy those quiet times out in the
5   backyard by myself.
6   I've seen a bunch of girls come and go these last four
7   years. That's the hardest part really. Saying goodbye to
8   new friends. Now it's my turn to go and I'm so scared.
9   This is the safest place I've ever been, how am I
10   supposed to leave it? Where am I supposed to go? I used
11   to dream of running away and being on my own and now
12   I'm scared to death! But Mr. and Mrs. Shores have
13   helped prepare me. They've set up my paperwork for
14   college and even put some money in the bank for me. I
15   know I should be excited ... and I am ... it's just so hard
16   to leave. For four years, this has been my family.

5. Bart and Lisa: You've Got to Be Kidding
(2 guys/1 girl)

Bart's Version

2 BART: I think kids should be allowed to sue their parents.
3   Sue them for all they've got and make them pay for being
4   such horrible, stupid parents! I'd take mine to the
5   cleaners, that's for sure.
6   See, a long time ago, my parents had a boy. They
7   named him Bart. That's me. Then, just two short years
8   later, they had a girl. They named her Lisa. Now at first
9   Bart and Lisa were two normal little kids who argued over
10   toys and spewed milk from their noses. Bart and Lisa
11   loved their parents and thought their parents loved them.
12   But Bart and Lisa grew up and Bart started going to
13   school. That's when Bart realized how his parents couldn't
14   have really loved him or they wouldn't have named him
15   after a *cartoon character!* Bart and Lisa? Come on!
16   Shouldn't that be considered a form of child abuse?
17   Naming your kid after a yellow-headed family? Were they
18   that unoriginal that they couldn't think up two perfectly
19   normal names? Something they didn't pick from a
20   television show?
21   Do you know how cruel kids can be? Shouldn't every
22   parent try their hardest to pick a name that won't cause
23   you to get beat up at school? Of course my mom and dad
24   have perfectly normal names: Phillip and Julie. How you
25   gonna make fun of that? Maybe that's why they were
26   completely clueless about picking out the stupidest
27   names on the planet.

1   I guess if Mom has another child it'll have to be named
2   Maggie! Probably even if it's a boy! Can I tell you that we
3   even have a cat named Snowball and a dog named
4   Santa's Little Helper! I'm serious! How whacked is that?
5   I think my parents are living in a fantasy world!
6   All my teachers just assume I'm a troublemaker like
7   my namesake. Why wouldn't they? You hear a name like
8   Bart and you want to run the other direction! And the real
9   troublemaker, Lisa, gets away with murder because
10   everyone thinks she's all sweet and innocent! *Not!*
11   I'm calling a lawyer right now. Somehow stupid
12   parents have got to be stopped! They've got to take this
13   kid-naming thing a little bit more seriously! I'm doing this
14   for you, future Maggie!
15
16   *Lisa's Version*
17 LISA: I have the coolest parents. You wouldn't think it to look
18   at them because they look like everybody else's parents.
19   Normal. Uptight. Parent-like. But they're not. They're
20   funny and crazy and don't care that they're more like
21   friends to us than parents. We have so much fun at our
22   house. My mom even helps my friends and me make
23   music videos! She helps set them up and then tapes
24   them for us. And my dad is nuts around my friends. Not
25   embarrassing nuts but fun nuts. He cracks them up with
26   stupid jokes or just acting crazy. They're like two kids
27   instead of two parents.
28   I guess that's why they thought it'd be fun to name my
29   brother and me after a fun TV family. My brother's Bart
30   and I'm Lisa. I think it's hilarious. Being named after a
31   drawing. Bart doesn't like it so much. In fact, the older
32   he gets, the more upset he seems to be about it all.
33   I think he was born out of a different mold than us
34   because he gets uptight about a lot of things. Like school
35   and stuff. God forbid he gets in trouble. I mean, he

1   practically cries and everything. It's like it's the end of
2   the world. He says teachers pick on him. So what, I say.
3   Pick back. That's what I do. And he says his friends
4   tease him all the time about being named Bart. What's
5   the big deal? I've heard of a lot worse names than that, I
6   can tell you.
7   Bart says he's going to sue Mom and Dad for naming
8   us Bart and Lisa. What a joke. I doubt a judge is going
9   to care about our names. It's not like they beat us. I don't
10   see why Bart is so upset in the first place. The character
11   Bart is cool. He's funny and popular and doesn't care
12   what other people think about him ... what's not to like
13   about being Bart?
14
15   *Father's Version*
16 FATHER: I guess we should have thought a little harder about
17   what to name our kids. It seemed so perfect at the time
18   though. It was my favorite TV show and we had a boy,
19   then a girl, and it was too good to pass up. We already
20   had the cat and the dog. Looking back, it probably was
21   insensitive to the kids. At least that's what Bart says. I
22   never meant to hurt him by naming him after the coolest
23   kid on TV. I figured there were far worse things. Like
24   naming him after Julie's grandfather: Walter Henry. What
25   kid wants an old-fashioned name like that? Bart was hip
26   and cool. And unique.
27   Bart sure doesn't think so. He's threatening to sue us.
28   As if the kid could get a lawyer! I just wish he could relax
29   about it all. He makes a bigger deal out of it than anyone.
30   If he didn't whine about it all the time, half the kids would
31   never even make the connection. Especially if they don't
32   know Lisa! Besides, he's had it this long, what's the big
33   deal now?
34   I'm starting to think we should've named *him* Lisa!
35   He's certainly more like her than Bart. Now, that would

1   be worse, wouldn't it? Having a girl's name? And there
2   are plenty of guys that I know that have girl-sounding
3   names! Jamie, Kim, Ashleigh. Now, that'd be something
4   to sue over, right?
5   I guess there's just one thing to do. Take him to the
6   courthouse and let him change his name. Let him see
7   how hard it is to come up with the *perfect* name for a kid.
8   I sure hate to see him do it though. Julie just found out
9   she's expecting and if, God willing, we had a girl, we were
10   planning on a little Maggie!

SECTION II
DUOLOGS

Dr. Jekyll and Mr. Hyde?

A single scene from two points of view.

6. So-Called Moms

(2 girls)

Kat's Version

2 KAT: I've got about ten so-called moms. See, I've been in
3   foster care since I was eight years old. They took my
4   brother and me from my mom because she was drunk all
5   the time. And 'cause one time we were home alone for
6   two days. I don't think anyone would've noticed except I
7   didn't go to school and they wondered where I was. But
8   how could I go and leave my baby brother at home alone?
9   I don't see what the big deal was. It was just two days.
10   I didn't miss that much school and besides, I've been
11   taking care of Andrew ever since he was born.
12   Everybody acted all shocked and concerned. Said an
13   eight-year-old can't be responsible for a baby. They paid
14   a lot of attention to me, telling me over and over that
15   things were going to get better. They even bought me a
16   doll. Like that was gonna help. They told me Andrew and
17   I were going to be OK. A bunch of lies. I don't even get
18   to see my brother any more. Is that their idea of OK?
19   We were together at first. They gave us to this family who
20   already had six kids. After only a couple of days there my
21   foster mom said I was too much trouble. She said I was in
22   her way too much trying to take care of Andrew. Can I help
23   it that she did everything wrong? She hardly ever changed
24   his diaper and she didn't feed him enough. See, Andrew
25   liked to eat a lot. I always gave him his bottle every time he
26   cried. She said crying was good for him. I think she was
27   just being stingy with the formula money. They get paid for
28   stuff like that. Anyway, she made them take me away.

1   Since then, I've been in eight other homes. I don't
2   seem to fit in. Everyone is always real nice at first. They
3   have their kids call me "sister" and the parents say I can
4   call them "Mom" and "Dad." That's a bunch of bull,
5   though, 'cause at the first sign of trouble, they're on the
6   phone getting me shipped out. Real parents don't do
7   that. Even Mom didn't want us to go. She cried when
8   they took us away. I just wish she'd stop drinking so that
9   we could go back home.
10   I miss my room even though I had to share it with
11   Andrew. And I miss taking care of him. I'm tired of
12   everyone telling me what to do. I'm old enough to be on
13   my own. I don't need some pseudo-family in my life. I get
14   my license soon and then I'm finding Andrew and
15   heading out. I practically raised him. He needs me and
16   not some family that only wants him so they can have the
17   money the state pays them.
18
19   *Mom #10's Version*
20 MOM #10: I don't know what to do about Kat. She's been
21   through so much in her life and I hate to let her down,
22   but I just don't know how to handle her. Deep down, I
23   think there's some goodness there but she won't let me
24   see it. Every time I think we're making a crack in that
25   hard shell of hers, she holes up in her room or does
26   something to get herself in trouble. I know she needs love
27   and understanding and I want to give that to her, but a
28   person can only take so much. How can you keep trying
29   to love someone who acts like they hate you?
30   Her file is about six inches thick. She's been shuffled
31   around for years. Maybe if her first placement ... or
32   second one ... or even her third one had worked out, she
33   wouldn't be so bitter now. How is anyone supposed to
34   deal with that? I know she's angry that she and Andrew
35   don't live together. I would be, too. I can't imagine being

1　separated from your sibling, especially when he's all you
2　had! But it's not my fault that things have turned out the
3　way they have. I'm trying to help her, but she can't even
4　see it. She thinks the whole world is out to get her and
5　I'm just one of them — one of those other mothers who
6　shipped her out without even giving her a chance.
7　　Well, I've given her a chance. Plenty of them and all she
8　does is throw them back in my face. How can I help
9　someone that doesn't want to be helped? I don't want to
10　send her back ... really, I don't. I just don't know how
11　much more my family can take. See, it's not just me
12　that's she's hurting. I thought maybe she'd be glad to have
13　a little brother again, not to take Andrew's place ... and
14　Kenton's so sweet ... how can she not at least like him a
15　little? But she won't even give him the time of day. He
16　wants so much for her to pay attention to him, but she
17　just walks right past him like he's invisible. His whole face
18　melts and he tries not to cry. I'm sick of her hurting him.
19　　It's so obvious. She's not looking for a family to love,
20　she's looking for a place to bide her time until she can be
21　on her own. Well, I don't want to be just a boarding
22　house for her. A place where she can keep her stuff until
23　that magical day when she turns eighteen. What does
24　she really think she's going to do then? She doesn't have
25　any money. Anywhere to go. She'll end up living on the
26　streets. Looking for a drugged-out mother that never
27　wanted her and certainly can't take care of her. We don't
28　want that for her. I wouldn't want that for anybody. But
29　how can I get her to believe me? She looks right through
30　me when I try to talk to her.
31　　I know what I have to do ...
32　　I'm sorry, Kat. I guess I'm no better than the other
33　nine so-called mothers you've had ... it's time for you to
34　go back.
35

7. Love?

(1 guy/1 girl)

1	*Keith's Version*

KEITH: OK. I can do this. I can say the "L" word. It's not that hard. I've said far worse four-letter words before, right? I'll just come right out with it, first thing, and get it over with. "Kelly," I'll say, "I love you." There. That wasn't so hard. I can say it to her face. I can. But what if she doesn't love me back? What if she just looks at me and says something like, "Thanks, what time are you picking me up tonight?"

What if she totally blows me off? I'll be standing there, looking all goofy, and she'll walk off laughing or something. Or she'll totally ignore that I said it and then I'll wonder if she even heard me or not.

Maybe I don't really love her. I mean, how can I be completely sure? I've never felt like this about anyone, but maybe it's just extreme liking. Not love. Just ... well, maybe lust ... 'cause she does have that great body and that sexy long hair that hangs down her back.

So what if I can't stop thinking about her. That doesn't have to be love, does it? Maybe I'm just obsessive compulsive. It does run in my family.

What was I thinking? I can't tell her I love her! Just because we've been dating over a year ... you can't put a time limit on these things! Maybe it takes two years to fall in love ... or three ... or maybe you have to be in college. Yeah. That sounds about right. High school kids can't be in love ... we're too young ... right?

But what if ... what if she's waiting for me to say it?

1   What if she breaks up with me just 'cause I don't say
2   that one little word? I'm gonna lose her ... I just know it.
3   OK. So I'm gonna tell her. I don't have to be *sure*, do
4   I? I can just say it and get it over with. It'll make her
5   happy. Here goes ... deep breath ...
6
7   *Kelly's Version*
8 KELLY: The worst thing in the world is about to happen and I
9   don't know how to stop it. My boyfriend, Keith, is about to
10   tell me that he loves me. The whole "I love you" phrase is
11   about to come out of his mouth and I don't know what to
12   do! Teresa said she heard him talking to Logan and today
13   is the day. You'd think I'd be ecstatic, but I'm not. I just
14   don't think I'm ready yet. So what am I supposed to say
15   back? I can't tell him that I love him if I don't! But I can't
16   just stand there either. It'll be so awkward! Then there will
17   be this whole thing between us and we'll probably end up
18   breaking up because things will be so weird!
19   Why is he rushing things like this? We're still so young.
20   I'm not ready for the kind of commitment that the "L"
21   word brings. I mean, I like him a lot, maybe I even do love
22   him, but I'm sure not ready to have that out there! I don't
23   take things like that lightly! Besides, what if he's just
24   saying it to move things along in other areas? I've heard
25   that guys will tell you anything to get what they want!
26   What if he's just saying it to get my guard down? What
27   if he thinks saying it means that I owe him something?
28   Ohmigosh! What am I gonna do? I like Keith so much.
29   We have a lot of fun together and we never fight or get
30   uncomfortable around each other. He's like my best
31   friend and this is going to ruin everything! We'll be like
32   those gross couples in school that are like, "I love you."
33   "No, I love *you*." "No, I love you *more*." It's disgusting!
34   Half the time they're all over each other with their
35   tongues halfway down each other's throats! If that's what

1　　　love is, I don't want it ... but I don't want to lose Keith ...
2　　　　　Oh no! Here he comes! He's got a funny look on his
3　　　face ... he's gonna do it ... I can tell ... what to do? What
4　　　to do?
5　　　　　I'm just gonna duck into the bathroom ... yeah ... I'll
6　　　wait till the bell rings ... he'll have to go to class without
7　　　me because he can't have any more tardies in fifth hour
8　　　or he's going to get detention ... that'll work ...
9　　　　　I wonder if he saw me ... what am I going to do about
10　　　next hour? He always waits for me ... oh, I think I'm going
11　　　to be sick ... maybe I'd better get Mom to pick me up ...
12　　　maybe by tomorrow he'll forget!

8. On the Net

(1 girl/1 guy)

Miranda's Version

MIRANDA: I just met the most wonderful guy! He's smart, funny, sweet, and so mature for a seventeen-year-old! We talked for hours last night and I would've talked to him all night except Mom made me get off the computer and go to bed.

I can't wait to get home from school today so that I can log on and see if he's there. I met him in this really great chat room for people with show dogs. We had so much to talk about! He's been raising show dogs for five years already! I'm just getting started so of course I have all kinds of questions! He's so smart! He knows everything!

The best part is he only lives about thirty miles away so one day we can meet! Oh, I know what everyone says about the dangers of meeting someone over the Net, and normally I'd agree. There are some real sickos out there, right? But I can tell that Stephen is totally on the up and up. Why would he lie, after all? He's a dog lover; I'm a dog lover. It's obvious that we were meant to meet each other. Who knows where it'll lead.

I tried telling my friend all about him, but she just kept saying negative things like, "He's probably a fat, bald fifty-year-old man hitting on a seventeen-year-old. Who says his name is even Stephen? It's probably Billy Bob and he only has three teeth or something."

I think she's just jealous because she doesn't have a boyfriend ... not that I'm calling Stephen my boyfriend ... not yet anyway ... we only met last night. But I have a really

1 good feeling about this. Sometimes you just gotta trust
2 your instincts, right? I'm sure I wouldn't be feeling this way
3 if he wasn't who he says ... I'd have a premonition or
4 something, right? And he would've slipped up somehow ...
5 I mean, we did talk for hours ... so what if he sounded older
6 than any guys I know — he's just smarter ... but what if ...
7 oh! I'm just being paranoid now! I know! I'll have him send
8 me a picture tonight! That'll clear everything up! I mean, a
9 picture can't lie, right?
10
11   *"Stephen's" Version*
12 "STEPHEN": Chat rooms have got to be the coolest invention
13 since the phone! I mean, either way you can't tell who's on
14 the other side, right? I love being able to talk to so many
15 people and not have to be face to face. It's not like I'm ugly
16 or anything ... I'm about average, I'd say, though I have
17 picked up a few pounds lately 'cause I've been sitting in
18 this chair night after night pounding away on this
19 keyboard! I'm just kind of shy. I've never been good at
20 meeting people. Just ask my wife. It took me almost a year
21 of being in her class, right beside her, before I finally asked
22 her out. Even then, she did most of the talking!
23   That's why the computer is so freeing! You can be
24 anybody you want to be. Or anything! Since I got hooked
25 on the Net, I've been a doctor, a lawyer, and a
26 schoolteacher. I even pretended to be a woman once,
27 just for the heck of it! You have to be careful, though,
28 'cause sometimes you can trip yourself up, throw out the
29 wrong medical term or something, and get caught red-
30 handed. But that's the beauty of it all; you just click your
31 way out and start again. No one ever knows.
32   Take last night for instance; I met this really funny
33 seventeen-year-old girl who has this insane love of dogs.
34 Well, my friend Tanner is a dog trainer who's been raising
35 show dogs for years. I used a couple of his "dog" phrases

1   and I was in like Flynn. We spent almost two hours
2   online. That's the great thing about my wife working
3   nights. She's never home during the good chat hours. I
4   have all night to meet who I want. And it's not as if I'm
5   hurting anyone. I mean, I'm just talking, right? I'm not
6   cheating on my wife or picking up some sleazeball at a
7   bar. I'm just having a plain, old conversation with a little
8   role-playing. Harmless. And I'm having the time of my
9   life. Where else can you be anybody you've ever dreamed
10   of being? I'm thinking of trying out the role of celebrity
11   one of these days! How fun would that be! Acting like
12   you've got it all. Being so ... adored. Why would anyone
13   ever want to be themselves? The world is wide open with
14   possibilities!

15   Of course, the downside is you can never meet these
16   people. Not face to face. I can just imagine old Miranda's
17   face if she were to walk up to a thirty-five-year-old man
18   instead of another seventeen-year-old dog lover! That'd
19   freak her out for sure! Of course, there's the possibility
20   that she's not who she says she is either! Maybe she's a
21   hundred-year-old grandma filling up her retirement years
22   hacking away on a computer. Who cares? I'm never gonna
23   meet her. Never gonna talk to her again. Although ...
24   she was awfully nice. Maybe I could meet her ... she
25   seemed open to it ... maybe she wouldn't even care that
26   I'm thirty-five ...

27   Nah. Tonight I'm moving on. Tonight I think I'll be ...
28   an astronaut ... or a fireman ... yeah! A fireman who
29   saved a little girl from a burning house and almost
30   died ... I can hardly wait!

9. Prom? No Way!
(1 guy/1 girl)

1   *Dennis' Version*

2   **DENNIS:** I feel lousy about the whole prom thing. I told my

3   girlfriend that I didn't want to go, made up some lame

4   excuse about not being able to dance (which is totally a

5   lie 'cause I can really kick butt on the dance floor) — and

6   now she's not talking to me.

7   I'm not a moron. I know how important the whole

8   prom thing is, and I'd really like to take her. I know she'd

9   look hot in a fancy dress with her hair all done up.

10   Problem is, I'm totally broke. I work twenty hours a week

11   bagging groceries and almost everything I make goes for

12   car insurance and gas. How am I supposed to pay for a

13   tuxedo rental, an expensive dinner, and a corsage? Oh,

14   and you have to have a highly overpriced prom photo,

15   too. You can't forget that!

16   It's so ridiculous to spend that kind of money on one

17   night! It'd take two paychecks, and even that probably

18   wouldn't be enough because some guys are talking about

19   limo rentals! I can't even imagine how much that would

20   cost me! It's so unfair that all of the cost of this "dream

21   night" falls on me ... and every other guy! The girls buy

22   a dress and they're done. We've got to fork over the cash

23   the whole night!

24   There's no way it could possibly be worth all that

25   money. It's not as if a tux is the most comfortable thing

26   to wear. I sure don't want to spend all night in one! And

27   having to dance on a crowded dance floor to some

28   crummy band or overage deejay. Oh yeah, I want to

1 spend my life's savings on that!
2   I just don't know how to tell Karen. If I tell her the
3 truth, she'll make me feel guilty for not wanting to spend
4 the money on her. She'll say I care more about the
5 almighty dollar than her! There's really no good way out
6 of it.
7   What if ... now, here's a thought ... what if I just agree
8 to it all and then prom night I just happen to get deathly
9 ill? Yeah ... that'd work, and she could never get mad
10 about that!
11   Hey! There she is! "Karen! Wait up! I've been thinking ... "
12
13   *Karen's Version*
14 KAREN: I can *not* believe this! I've waited my whole entire life
15 for this and now Dennis is backing out? I'm so mad I can
16 barely think! I feel like punching him in the face and I've
17 never hit a soul in my life! But that's how angry I am.
18 Prom night is like one of the most important nights in
19 any girl's life and he's trying to take that from me! It's
20 right up there with getting married! From the time I've
21 been a little girl I've imagined myself in a million different
22 dresses and with a million different guys and now that
23 I've got a boyfriend and wouldn't dream of going with
24 anyone else — I can't go? I don't think so!
25   Dennis cannot take this from me! It's my Cinderella
26 night! How can he be so selfish as to come up with some
27 lame "I can't even dance" excuse! Does he think I'm an
28 idiot? I've seen him dance before and he does just fine.
29 Well, if he thinks I'm going to miss my senior prom just
30 because he doesn't want to go, he's out of his mind!
31 What is his problem anyway? Is he embarrassed to go
32 with me? Is this his way of getting me to break up with
33 him? What's the deal?
34   I'd ask him, but I haven't said a word to him since he
35 told me. I knew if I opened my mouth then I was going to

1　let loose! But he knows I'm mad. I've been glaring at him
2　ever since, and when I calm down (*if* I ever calm down!)
3　I'm going to tell him exactly what I think about him bailing
4　on me. I think I'll even have another date lined up, just to
5　show him that he can't just carelessly ruin my life!

6　　I know there are plenty of guys that don't have dates
7　yet. In fact, there's a guy in next hour who I know would
8　go with me in a heartbeat. He's been asking me all year
9　when I was going to break up with Dennis. Well, I guess
10　now's the time because I'm sure not going to go to prom
11　by myself! And I can't go with another guy if I'm dating
12　Dennis!

13　　I just can't believe he's being so heartless! To take
14　this night away so casually as if it's not a big deal is
15　totally unforgivable! It just shows how self-centered he
16　is, not even thinking about how it would make me feel. I
17　don't care if does think he can't dance, he could dance
18　like a troll and I wouldn't care! I just want to go! With
19　him! I want my night of memories! Memories you only get
20　one shot at! Doesn't he get it?

10. She Hates Me
(2 girls)

1   *Amanda's Version*

2   AMANDA: My teacher hates me. It's true. I'm not

3   exaggerating. I can be sitting there doing nothing,

4   minding my own business, and she'll call me down for

5   something stupid like tapping my foot or twirling my hair.

6   Something completely off the wall.

7   "Earth to Amanda," she'll say. "Come back to us." As

8   if I'm some kind of airhead that can't stay focused in class.

9   If I am daydreaming it's only because she's the most

10   boring teacher on the planet. Can I help it if sometimes

11   my mind wanders and all I can think of is being anywhere

12   but in her stinking class?

13   There's one girl who never does her work, comes in

14   tardy just about every other day, and sometimes takes a

15   nap through class. Does she get yelled at? I don't think

16   so. Wanna know why? She's the teacher's pet. I think she

17   even baby-sits for Mrs. Ryan or something. She gets

18   away with murder and I get called for breathing too hard!

19   I swear!

20   One time I was all stuffed up and I let out a huge sigh,

21   you know, just a release of air, and guess what she

22   said — "Am I boring you, Amanda? Maybe you'd like to

23   teach the class."

24   Well, maybe I would. I could do way better than her,

25   that's for sure. And I wouldn't pick on kids just for the

26   heck of it. I'd be known as the fairest teacher in school.

27   No playing favorites for me. Equality, that's what I say.

28   Everyone treated exactly the same. Even the stuck-up

1   prissy ones that waltz into class late and then sleep

2   through the lesson. Well ... I may have to pick on them a

3   little ... but come on, *they* deserve it! I don't!

4

5   *Mrs. Ryan's Version*

6 MRS. RYAN: I am so frustrated about Amanda Miller. She

7   has the potential to be the best student in class and yet

8   day after day I see her barely putting forth the effort to

9   even pay attention. She thinks the bare minimum is

10   acceptable on everything and doesn't step out of that

11   "average" box that everyone seems to have put her in. No

12   one expects her to excel, so she doesn't.

13   But she has it in her. I know she does. I've seen

14   glimpses of it in her work — brief glimmers of something

15   much more than the C student she appears to be.

16   She reminds me of me when I was her age. I sat in

17   class and did only what I had to do to get by. My parents

18   were already invested in my straight-A sister so they

19   didn't expect much from me. I guess we all knew I

20   couldn't compete with her. Still, it would've been nice if

21   they at least acted like I could've been in the same league.

22   I guess that's why I'm a little hard on Amanda. I can tell

23   she thinks I'm picking on her. Man, can she ever give me

24   a look! But I'm hoping to crack into that shell of hers.

25   Spark some kind of desire to be more than average.

26   Someone who excels in life and doesn't just get by. It's

27   probably unfair, but I've invested some kind of hope in her

28   and I'm not willing to give up. I wish she could understand

29   that I'm not being mean. I want what's best for her. I want

30   her to see that she can be more than average.

31

32

33

34

35

11. Betrayal
(2 girls)

1   *Alicia's Version*

2   ALICIA: I can't believe Sidney. I thought I could trust her.

3   We've been friends since third grade! She was the first

4   person I met when I moved here and nothing has ever

5   come between us. We've gone through everything

6   together — her parents getting divorced, my dog dying,

7   her sister being in the hospital. I mean, we've got serious

8   history! Which is why I thought I could trust her with

9   anything. Even my deepest, weirdest thoughts. I never

10   dreamed she'd turn on me this way.

11   It was just a stupid comment — one I made to her

12   when she spent the night this weekend — and now she's

13   spread it all over school. Like it's a fact. She's told

14   everyone I'm gay and she's acting like she doesn't even

15   know me anymore.

16   Well, for the record, I am *not* gay. Here's what

17   happened: we were talking about all kinds of stupid stuff

18   and I happened to say that I wondered what it would be

19   like to kiss a girl instead of a guy. I didn't say I *wanted*

20   to. I mean, you see it all over TV, and it just made me

21   wonder, if you're *not* gay and you do it — are you totally

22   grossed out? Or does it feel any different since most

23   times you have your eyes closed anyway? It's not that I

24   was saying I wanted to try it. I swear. I was just curious

25   about it. Who wouldn't be as much as we're bombarded

26   by it? TV makes it seem so natural, like it's no big deal,

27   so I was just wondering if a person like me — one who

28   likes *guys,* did it — would it feel strange or wrong?

1   But none of that matters because according to the
2   whole school I'm gay now. Everything I've ever done —
3   hugged a friend hello — has been exaggerated and made
4   to seem like a "sign." It's ridiculous and I've lost my best
5   friend ever. She knows me better than anyone. How
6   could she even think such a thing? Much less spread it
7   around school? She should be standing up for me, not
8   promoting all this!
9   Maybe I should just "let it slip" that ever since her
10   parents split up, she's been sleeping in her mother's
11   room. Surely there's something sick about that? Right?
12   Or maybe I'll tell everyone about her wearing *boys*
13   boxers! Or that in seventh grade she stuffed her bra with
14   toilet paper and lied to everyone about starting her period
15   when she didn't really start until two years later!
16   See, I've got plenty of dirt on her, too! By the end of
17   the day, she'll be sorry she ever knew me!
18
19   *Sidney's Version*
20 SIDNEY: Things have gotten way out of hand. I knew better
21   than to tell Patsi anything. I knew she wouldn't keep it to
22   herself. But it kind of just slipped out. I mean, come on,
23   you have to admit the whole thing is kind of weird. What
24   Alicia said to me the other night. How was I supposed to
25   keep that to myself?
26   Still, I never dreamed it would spread like wildfire
27   around school. Practically everyone has come up to me
28   at some point and asked me if Alicia's gay. Of course I
29   tell them no because I know she's not. But I can tell they
30   don't believe me. They think I'm covering for her since
31   she's my best friend and all.
32   Or should I say she was. I doubt she'll ever talk to me
33   again. I can't blame her. I'd be pretty mad, too. But I feel
34   really bad about it and I'd do anything to make it up to
35   her. The thing is, if I act too chummy with her now people

1   will think I'm gay, too. I don't know if I can handle that.
2   Alicia's thicker-skinned than me. She says she doesn't
3   care a rat's tail whether people like her or not. Well, I do.
4   It bothers me, drives me crazy, if someone acts like they
5   don't like or are mad at me. I could never stand for the
6   whole school to be gossiping about me! I'd need serious
7   therapy to cope with something like that! But Alicia's not
8   like me. She doesn't care. This probably isn't even
9   getting to her all that much.

10   So maybe I'll give her a little space — to cool off for a
11   while — and to let the rumors die down. Then, I'll make
12   it up to her somehow. I swear.

13   After all, we've been best friends forever!

12. Share and Share Alike

(2 guys)

1   *Joe's Version*

2   JOE: I've been stealing from my brother. Not a lot. Just a five-

3   dollar bill every now and then. But I feel horrible about it.

4   I know he works hard for his money. Geesh, he complains

5   about it enough for us all to know how bad his job is. And

6   I know I shouldn't take money that isn't mine, but in my

7   defense, he's always just leaving it lying around. Top of

8   his dresser, on the bathroom counter, even on the floor

9   — everywhere! It's like he just empties his pockets

10   anywhere and then scoops it back into another pair of

11   pants whenever he needs it. Hasn't he ever heard of a

12   wallet? I mean, if it wasn't staring me in the face all the

13   time, I might not be so tempted to take it. I'm not the

14   kind of person that would actually go *looking* for money

15   that wasn't mine. Flipping through a wallet and actually

16   taking money out ... now that's wrong!

17   He just makes it so easy. It's like he doesn't care

18   about the money, the way he leaves it lying all over the

19   place, so why not take a little every now and then? He's

20   not going to miss it! And if he did, as careless as he is,

21   he'd probably just think he'd lost it somewhere. Which,

22   by the way, is a huge possibility. How many times has

23   Mom given him wrinkled up bills from the washer or

24   dryer? So what's the difference if the dryer gets it or I do?

25   He should keep up with it better.

26   Well ... I know it's not his fault. I'm not completely

27   immoral. The money's not mine and I shouldn't take it.

28   Simple as that. He'd probably even give me some ... if I

1   asked. It's just easier this way. He doesn't seem to miss
2   it and I don't have to grovel. Works for both of us.
3   Maybe I'll buy him something nice to make up for it.
4   He's been wanting this new CD ... I could probably afford
5   it if I just took a ten-dollar bill this time instead of a five.
6   I've still got a few bucks left over from last week ... he
7   never spends money on himself ... it'd be a real treat for
8   him. That's it. I've made up my mind. He's going to be
9   so thankful when he sees what I've done!
10
11   *Richard's Version*

12 RICHARD: I don't know what to do about my brother, Joe. I
13   think he's doing drugs or something because he's always
14   stealing money from me. I mean, he's got to be pretty
15   desperate to steal from his own brother, right? I figure he
16   must be in pretty bad. But I don't know how to approach
17   him about it. I keep hoping he'll trust me enough to come
18   to me with his problem. He knows I'm here for him. But I'm
19   afraid if I confront him, he'll just steal from someone ... or
20   somewhere else! The last thing I want is for my brother to
21   end up in jail!
22   He's not stealing a lot of money, so maybe it's not too
23   bad. Maybe it's cigarettes or something and not drugs.
24   Not that I want him smoking either, but at least that'd be
25   easier to deal with. He can't be doing too much of
26   anything because he's not stealing a lot of money. He only
27   takes about five dollars a week. Sometimes a little more.
28   He'd need a whole lot more than that if he was into the
29   hard stuff, right? I have no idea how much drugs cost! But
30   what if he's already stealing from other people ... maybe
31   Mom ... no, surely he wouldn't take money from Mom! He
32   knows how hard it is for her right now. We barely have
33   grocery money! That would really make me mad if he was
34   stealing from her!
35   I guess I'm going to have to talk to him. Find out

1   what's going on. It's my duty as his big brother, right?
2   Maybe it's not so bad. Maybe we can nip this thing in the
3   bud and Mom will never have to know. She's got so much
4   on her shoulders already.
5   Tonight when I get off work, I'm gonna have a long talk
6   with Joe. I just hope he'll come clean. I'd hate to think
7   he's a thief *and* a liar.

13. *My* Daughter?!
(1 girl/1 guy)

Mother's Version

2   MOTHER: I just can't believe it. I can't. My hands are shaking

3   so badly I can barely drive. I couldn't even tell my boss

4   what was wrong, just grabbed my purse and ran out. How

5   am I going to explain to everyone at work that the child I

6   brag about all the time, my A-plus student who wins

7   awards for Pete's sake, has just been caught shoplifting?

8   She baby-sits for my friends! How are they going to feel

9   about having a thief watch their children? She'll probably

10   never work again, but that's the least of my problems!

11   How could I have missed this? I thought Paige was on

12   the right track. Doing all the right things. Making all the

13   right choices. She goes to youth group at church every

14   Wednesday night! Hangs out with good kids ... well,

15   mostly. I worry some about Candy. She seems all innocent

16   and sweet, but there's something sneaky about her.

17   Maybe she had something to do with this! Paige would

18   never have come up with this on her own ... would she?

19   I just don't know. You think you're connected with

20   your children and then, wham! Something like this

21   happens. I thought I knew her. Knew who she was. How

22   could she do this? She knows all the horrible things that

23   her sister has put me through. Is that why she's acting

24   out now? For attention?

25   Oh, it's all my fault. I've been working too much lately.

26   Who knows what she's been up to while I've been at the

27   office. Maybe drinking ... doing drugs. I should've known

28   better than to take that promotion. I knew it would mean

1   more hours, and now look what's happened. My daughter
2   has stolen something to get my attention! How could I
3   have been so stupid? After Kim, I should've been on the
4   lookout. Should've checked her things. Searched her
5   room. I should've never trusted that she wasn't into the
6   wrong things ... right?
7   But Paige has always been so open ... so honest ...
8   Has all that been an act and I've played right into her
9   hands? Giving her much more freedom than Kim ever
10   had. I guess that's it. I've been tricked by her sweet face,
11   good grades, and friendship. I thought we told each other
12   everything. I guess I was wrong. I shouldn't have trusted
13   my gut. That's when you get into trouble, right? A
14   mother's intuition isn't always right, is it? Because I
15   never saw this coming! So what kind of mother does that
16   make me? Obviously a very stupid one. As soon as I get
17   this straightened out, I'm keeping her under lock and
18   key! I will not have another child of mine going down the
19   wrong path. I hope Paige enjoyed her freedom, because
20   all of that is about to end!
21

22   *Security Guard's Version*
23 SECURITY GUARD: I see this kind of thing all the time and
24   I'm sick of the drama. Poor pitiful little girl crying in the
25   office because she got her hand caught in the cookie jar!
26   What makes me sick is almost every time the kid has
27   enough money to buy the thing they're ripping off, so
28   what makes them do it? Kids today have a lot more
29   luxuries than I ever had and they still feel the need to
30   steal more? Pampered little brats that think the world
31   owes them everything!
32   They're all cocky in the store ... before they get
33   caught. Rude to the checkout clerks. Knocking stuff off
34   displays and never dreaming of picking them up. Yeah,
35   they even got attitude right up until the point I walk them

1   back here. Then they pipe down a little. Get all quiet and
2   thoughtful, probably planning their lies about how they
3   didn't really mean to steal it ... they were going to pay for
4   it ... blah, blah, blah. Bunch of liars.
5   Then when they realize their lame story isn't getting
6   them anywhere, that's when the tears start. I've had
7   some real bawlers back here. Some you'd think were
8   dying, they cry so hard. But it's all an act. I'm not stupid.
9   They don't have an ounce of remorse for doing it, only
10   for getting caught. They think if they cry hard enough, I'll
11   let them go. Give them some kind of lame warning or
12   threaten to call their parents or, better yet, the police and
13   then let them go out of the kindness of my heart.
14   Well, here's the part they don't know. I don't have any
15   kindness left. I've been watching punks rip off this store
16   for years and I'm sick of it. This store doesn't owe them
17   anything and neither do I. If they want some kind of
18   cheap thrill, go ride a roller coaster or jump out of a
19   plane. We're not here to provide some kind of rush. We're
20   here to sell products and make money. I'm here to make
21   a living. Maybe these lazy kids might want to try that
22   sometime. Actually work for something.
23   So do I feel sorry for little Miss Goody Two Shoes who
24   swears she never stole anything before in her life? Not an
25   ounce. She got herself here all on her own. She put the
26   polish in her purse. Her own grubby little fingers. If she
27   doesn't want to be treated like a thief, then don't be one.
28   Next time, take some of that cash out of your purse, plop
29   it down on the counter, and pay for that neon bottle of
30   polish you stashed. And maybe, just maybe, you could
31   even smile at the clerk and say thank you ... but now I'm
32   really dreaming, aren't I?
33
34
35

14. The Slap
(2 girls)

1   *Melanie's Version*

2   MELANIE: I never thought she'd slap me. Not on the face like

3   that. When I was little, she smacked my bottom or even

4   the side of my leg. But never this. Never on the face. So

5   how could I have prepared myself for it? I couldn't.

6   I can feel her hand against my cheek. The skin is still

7   stinging. I'm sure it's red. Not because she hit me that

8   hard but because I still feel the shame of it all. Why had

9   I said that to her? I knew of all things what I said would

10   hurt her the most.

11   "Fine. I'll just go live with Dad then," I said, just like

12   that, snotty and disrespectful like that's what she

13   deserved even though I knew she didn't. I saw the look

14   in her eyes. First shock, then deep hurt. I know it's why

15   she lashed out. She wanted to hurt me back.

16   She hadn't deserved those words. She was protecting

17   me, trying to help me make the right decision. But I

18   didn't see it. I saw her as controlling. Unrelenting. I was

19   angry. And stupid. We both knew there was no way I'd

20   ever leave to live with my father. Not even a remote one.

21   He wouldn't want me and I wouldn't want to go. It was a

22   horrible threat. A horrible thanks to my mom who had

23   done so much for me.

24   I would've immediately taken the words back but

25   then came the slap. It shocked us both into silence and

26   then Mom ran from the room. I knew I should go after

27   her, to apologize, but I couldn't. I felt rooted there.

28   Unable to move.

1   Now there's this — this huge thing hanging between
2   us. My words broke her trust; her slap destroyed mine. I
3   wish we could both take them back. Start the argument
4   over and this time I'd listen. I wouldn't say those awful
5   words and she wouldn't slap my face. I wouldn't be afraid
6   of her ...
7
8   *Mother's Version*
9   MOTHER: I don't know how I'll ever face my daughter again.
10   I did the stupidest thing a mother can do. I slapped my
11   daughter. Not hard, but that's really not the point. I hit
12   her and I can never forgive myself. Especially given our
13   family history. My ex-husband was such a mean man.
14   Melanie was always terrified of him. I never wanted her to
15   feel that way about me. She knew ... knows ... I'd never
16   hurt her on purpose. But now how is she supposed to
17   believe that?
18   Running away from her wasn't the answer. I know that.
19   I was just too upset to stay. Too shocked that I had let
20   my anger get the better of me. Her words were cruel, but
21   I know Melanie well enough to know she didn't mean
22   them. We've been in this together since the beginning.
23   She wouldn't bail on me now. Besides, live with her dad?
24   What a joke. She'd have to find him first.
25   So why did I do it? Why did I hit this person I love with
26   all my heart? Am I no better than my ex? Oh, I hope
27   that's not true. What if she tells someone? Will they take
28   her away from me? Even if she doesn't want to go ... but
29   what if she does? What if she's afraid of me now? Thinks
30   that I'm going to hit her like her dad used to ... oh, I
31   couldn't bear for her to think that.
32   I've got to go talk to her. Tell her how sorry I am. I'll
33   do whatever it takes. Go to counseling. Take an anger
34   management class. She just has to know how sorry I
35   am. Melanie, I never meant to hurt you.

15. Chicken of the Sea
(2 girls)

1   *Chloe's Version*

2 CHLOE: I am scared to death of the ocean. Truly petrified to

3   even put my feet in. But I wasn't always like that. I used

4   to swim and raft and snorkel and do all the fun things

5   other people do in the ocean. That was before. Before the

6   day I stepped smack dab on a stingray and the sucker

7   stuck me with his tail! Right down into the bone of my

8   foot! Of course at the time, I had no idea what happened.

9   All I knew was I've never had such pain in my life! I

10   started screaming bloody murder. I know everyone

11   thought a shark had started to eat me! I come hobbling

12   out of the ocean, my mom takes one look at my foot and

13   says, "It's just a scratch. What are you screaming

14   about?" I swear I wanted to punch her! It might've been

15   a scratch on the outside, but inside it was pure agony!

16   She took me inside, mostly because I think she was

17   embarrassed for everyone to see me carrying on that

18   way, and then do you know what my brilliant mother did?

19   Had my sister pee in a cup so she could pour it on my

20   foot! Gross! She'd heard somewhere that urine helped

21   jellyfish stings, which is what she thought got me. To tell

22   the truth, I was in so much pain, I didn't care. I would've

23   drunk it, if I thought it would've helped! (OK, maybe not,

24   but I really was in pain!)

25   My mom called this help number on the fridge and

26   they said they could tell by my screaming that I'd been

27   stung by a stingray. See — they knew how bad it hurt!

28   The doctor even said that it can make grown men cry

1   and I was just a little girl!

2   Anyway, we got to the urgent treatment place. They

3   put my foot in ice (not *hot* water, *Mom!*) and then

4   gave me shots for the pain. They even had these little

5   patches with pain medicine built right in. Now those

6   things were wonderful! Oh, and the doctor was really hot,

7   too, so that helped a little. But not enough to convince

8   me to try it again.

9   To this day I'm afraid to get in the ocean and no one

10   understands it. "Do the stingray shuffle." "It's not going

11   to happen again." What do they know? I'm the kind of

12   person that things like this *do* happen to over and over

13   again! Or maybe there is a shark out there just waiting

14   to get a taste of me! Call me chicken, I don't care! All I

15   know is that there ain't *no* creatures in the pool!

16

17   *Mother's Version*

18 MOTHER: You can't blame me for not believing that Chloe

19   was in serious pain. All I saw was a teeny little scratch

20   on the top of her foot. I thought maybe a seashell had

21   scratched her or at the worst a little crab. But there she

22   was, screaming her head off, all the way back up to the

23   condo. I think people thought I was beating her or

24   something! Believe me, I was thinking about it! At first.

25   Then I saw that she really was in a lot of pain. I

26   remembered this show about jellyfish stings, so we

27   poured pee all over her foot. Didn't work. We tried hot

28   water, didn't work. Cold water. Didn't work. I was running

29   out of ideas and she was still crying hysterically. The

30   scratch was starting to swell into a whitish-looking lump.

31   I called this number on the fridge — apparently this

32   stuff happens pretty often down here — and they told me

33   to bring her in right away. By then we knew what it was

34   that got her — stingray. Suddenly, I was much more

35   sympathetic. I felt horrible for giving her a hard time at

1   first. Luckily, she was in so much pain, she forgave me!

2   She perked up pretty quick when this hot, tan doctor

3   walked into the room. She didn't even freak out about

4   the shots like she normally would have. Took them like a

5   brave young woman who was flirting her little head off.

6   Thank God for cute doctors!

7   Anyway, she made it through. Suffered a few

8   complications later but survived. Now I can't get her back

9   in the ocean. She's scared to death another stingray's

10   out to get her! Even though we all know now that they

11   only strike when you step on them. You just gotta do the

12   stingray shuffle and they'll swim as far away as possible.

13   I don't know what to do to convince her! They even had

14   this girl on TV who had her arm bit off by a shark and

15   she still swims in the ocean! But Chloe's not budging. I

16   guess our beach days are over. Unless ... hey, Chloe ...

17   look at that cute guy getting on that surfboard ... maybe

18   you should go talk to him ...

16. Green-Eyed Monster
(1 girl/1 guy)

1   *Kayla's Version*

2 KAYLA: My boyfriend is so jealous. It's downright ridiculous! It

3   used to be kind of cute, but now I can't stand it. I can't

4   even talk to another guy without him totally flipping out.

5   He thinks every boy I pass in the hall is checking me out!

6   Get real! I'm not the ugliest girl in the school, but I'm sure

7   not model material. I seriously doubt anyone even notices

8   me! But not according to James. You wouldn't believe how

9   many times he's told some poor unsuspecting soul to

10   "move along, ain't nothing to see here."

11   My point exactly! I mean, it's sweet that he apparently

12   thinks I'm beautiful, but I'm not dumb enough to think

13   everyone else does! And even if they did? So what? It's

14   not like I'm scoping out my options. I love James. I want

15   to be with him. Why can't he stop being so paranoid that

16   someone's going to steal me away! Because he's going

17   to *drive* me away if he doesn't stop!

18   He even accuses me of flirting when we go out to eat.

19   Says I'm way too friendly with the guy in the so-cute

20   (*not!*) polyester uniform who takes my order! Yeah, right!

21   I'm just a friendly person. Can I help that?

22   Well, he's just gonna have to get over his insecurities

23   'cause I'm sick of it. He makes me feel like I'm loose or

24   something, always on the prowl, and I haven't even done

25   anything wrong!

26   The latest thing is absolutely out-of-this-world crazy.

27   He's upset over a movie star! I made the mistake of

28   telling him how hot I thought this guy was on my mom's

1   favorite soap and now he's acting all mad and hurt!
2   Saying maybe I should be with him! Ha! Like I'd ever
3   have *that* chance! I guess I'm not supposed to even
4   admire anyone from afar. Even a guy that's twice, maybe
5   even three times, my age!
6   It's a good thing he's not allowed one step in my
7   bedroom because he'd flip over my boy band posters that
8   are all over the walls! It's my one place I can sit back and
9   dream and *not* be accused of cheating! It's horrible being
10   with the Green-Eyed Monster!
11
12   *James' Version*
13 JAMES: My girlfriend is a huge flirt. No matter where we go,
14   she's always checking other guys out. Right in front of
15   me! When I point it out to her, she gets mad. Gives me
16   that line of bull about "just being friendly." Baloney.
17   "Just being a flirt" is more like it. I don't understand why
18   she can't see it.
19   I'm not being paranoid either. I swear. Even my friends
20   tell me that she flirts with them. My friends! How low is
21   that? I can't even leave her alone with my friends for fear
22   that she's going to come on to them. I wonder how she'd
23   like it if I flirted with *her* friends the way she does with
24   mine. She'd probably cause a big scene and make me feel
25   like a horrible low-life who can't be trusted!
26   That's what she says I do with her. But I don't. I trust
27   her. I do. I'm just sick of seeing her bat her pretty blue
28   eyes at every guy alive. Why can't she just focus on me
29   for a change? Am I that bad looking that she has to
30   scope out her options twenty-four/seven? I may not be a
31   Calvin Klein model, but I do work out. I don't think I'm
32   that bad to look at. Surely, she can drag her eyes off
33   everyone else every now and then to at least notice me!
34   I just don't know what to do about her. I care about
35   her a lot. And I think she actually cares about me, too.

1   It's almost like this disease she has! Flirtitis, or
2   something! I don't even think she knows she does it half
3   the time! So maybe she can't really control it. And if she
4   can't control it, then I guess I shouldn't hold it against
5   her ... I'll just have to look the other way ... pretend not
6   to see her smiling at those other guys ... ignore ... oh,
7   who am I kidding? I'm just too jealous to be with a flirt!

17. BB Guns — You Call That Fun?

(2 guys)

1   *Clinton's Version*

2 CLINTON: My friends are idiots! Complete and total out-of-

3   their-minds idiots! I always knew they were a little off but

4   I had no idea they'd come up with something this stupid!

5   See, we all went over to Neil's farm on Friday night for a

6   big bonfire where we were going to camp out all night.

7   Roast some hot dogs. Maybe a couple bags of

8   marshmallows. You know, typical outdoorsy kind of stuff.

9   But no! That's not enough for these guys. We hadn't

10   been there two hours when someone starts passing out

11   the BB guns from the back of Neil's truck.

12   At first I didn't think anything of it. Thought maybe we

13   were going to do a little target shooting ... I'm not totally

14   anti-gun, after all. But now that I think about it, I

15   should've known that would've been too lame for these

16   guys ... oh no ... they didn't want to shoot at paper or

17   cans ... they wanted to shoot at each other!

18   "Are you crazy?" I said after Neil started breaking us up

19   into "war" teams. "You want us to *shoot* at each *other?*" My

20   voice screeched like a girl's but I was too scared to care.

21   "It's no big deal," my friend Seth said. "We do this all

22   the time."

23   They did? How come I'd never known that? I guess

24   they'd always done it without me. I was starting to

25   understand why my friends were practically straight F

26   students! They were stupid! It was all so clear.

27   "It only hurts for a second," Neil chimed in. "Just a

28   little sting when the pellet hits you."

1   They stood staring at me. Stings. That didn't sound so
2   bad. I mean, if they did it all the time ... a "do it, don't
3   do it" battle raged in my head while they stood there
4   watching, waiting to see if I'd wimp out. What was I
5   supposed to do? I grabbed a gun and took off running. I
6   figured I could always hide behind a tree all night.
7   And my plan worked for a while. Until Seth came from
8   behind and started shooting at me! A little sting, my foot!
9   When one of those bullets hits you, it hurts! I could feel
10   welts rising up on my back and legs. I took off running.
11   All night I ran and hid. Not once did I fire the stupid
12   gun in my hands.
13   Not once.
14   Which is how I know for sure that it was not me who
15   shot Neil Sharp in the face that night.
16   It was not me who made him lose his eye.
17
18   *Neil's Version*
19   NEIL: I just wish I knew who did it. Who was stupid enough to
20   shoot me in the face? Because of that moron, I've got to
21   go around with this stupid-looking fake eye for the rest of
22   my life! I know it wouldn't bring my eye back, but I sure
23   would have a thing or two to say to that stupid jerk! Who
24   could possibly be dumb enough to aim high like that?
25   I'll tell you who it was. Clinton. I knew we never
26   should've invited him that night. We never had before
27   because we knew how he was. Chicken. I don't know
28   what made us cave and invite him then. You could tell he
29   was shocked when we started handing out the BB guns.
30   His face was completely white. I thought maybe he was
31   going to pee his pants! Then, when we explained the
32   game, he could barely speak, he was so terrified!
33   That's why I know it was Clinton who shot me. He was
34   so scared he probably shot at everything that moved that
35   night. Probably hid behind a tree and fired off shots like

a crazy man. Didn't aim. Didn't even look. Probably didn't even know how to really shoot a gun. Nobody thought to even ask if he did.

Now I've lost an eye and it's all his fault. We played war plenty of times before and nobody got hurt. Oh, we got some pretty good welts, but nobody went blind! It was all perfectly fine until yellow Clinton showed up. Even now he won't be a man and admit that he shot me. Tries to say he didn't even fire his gun! Yeah, right. Like we're supposed to believe someone as scared stiff as him wouldn't be tight on the trigger! He just stood there and took it! I may be half blind but I'm not stupid! Oh, it was Clinton all right, and one day I'm gonna make him pay for it.

18. Blind Date
(1 guy/1 girl)

Joey's Version
2   JOEY: I don't think I've ever been so nervous in my life. Here
3   I am, getting ready to knock on the door of a girl I've
4   never even met. Never even spoken with. In just a few
5   short minutes I'm going to see this girl I've got to spend
6   the next five hours with. Who knows what she looks
7   like ... or what we'll talk about. Why did I ever let my
8   cousin hook me up? I know the horror stories of blind
9   dates. How could I have been so stupid? This girl's gonna
10   think I'm desperate ... that I can't get a date on my own.
11   She's probably dreading this as much as I am! Who
12   knows how Anna even talked her into it. What favor did
13   she have to call in to arrange this?
14   But what if she's not dreading it? What if she's been
15   looking forward to this all day? Maybe she's imagining me
16   to be some knight in shining armor or something like that
17   and then she sees this? I mean, come on, I'm not Prince
18   Charming! How can anyone live up to an expectation like
19   that?! Who knows what Anna told her. Maybe she lied
20   about me. Told her I'm some jock or something. Maybe I
21   should just bail now before she sees me ...
22   Oh, no! I think I just saw her peeking through the
23   windows. I've gone blank. I can't even remember her name!
24   What do I do now? I can't run and jump back in the car.
25   Anna would kill me! I mean, this is her friend, after all ...
26   think, Joey, think. Maybe I could say I got sick ... you know,
27   on the drive over ... carsickness ... yeah, that's it. I can
28   look all ill and hunched over when she opens the door ...

1   She's here. The door's opening.

2   Well, her feet aren't so bad. Small. Cute little heels.

3   Ankle bracelet. Tan legs. But you never know …

4   I moan a little and clutch my stomach.

5   "Are you OK?" she asks and her hand flutters against

6   my arm. Like a soft butterfly. Her voice is sweet and

7   harmonic. I stay hunched over, not sure what to do. Bail

8   or take the plunge? Seriously, was there really hope for

9   any blind date? Ever?

10   "Are you sick?" she asks again, and this time I look

11   up at her face to answer. It's the face of an angel. I

12   swear. And concern, real concern, shows on her face.

13   The plan in my head flies with the wind. I straighten up

14   quickly, "Oh, I'm fine. Just had a little carsickness,

15   that's all. It's like that sometimes. Usually passes pretty

16   fast. Ready to go?"

17   "In the car?" she asks with a funny look on her face

18   and I realize my mistake. The beautiful girl with the round

19   blue eyes staring at me thinks I'm going to puke all over

20   her! What do I do now? Oh, I knew this was never gonna

21   work! I can't tell if that look on her face is fear of vomit

22   or fear of me! What a disaster! I'm outta here!

23

24   *Veronica's Version*

25 VERONICA: I always knew I wasn't drop-dead gorgeous but I

26   never thought I was ugly enough to make a guy run away

27   from me! I could just kill Anna for setting this up in the first

28   place! Joey must've thought I was desperate before he even

29   met me. And apparently I should be! He took one look at

30   me and practically turned green!

31   I've never felt so bad in my whole life. It's like I was

32   jilted at the altar! I just stood there like the biggest dork

33   on earth while the guy jumped in his car and drove off!

34   And don't think for a minute that I bought his line about

35   carsickness! What a crock! He took one look at me and

1   was ready to puke. That's sure to make a person feel
2   special. Look at me! Do I really induce people to
3   vomiting? Should I be going through life with a paper bag
4   over my head? Did I have food in my teeth or something
5   awful like that?
6   Well, he can just drive on off in his stupid little
7   convertible sports car. Anyone who drives something like
8   that is obviously too egocentric for me anyhow. I don't
9   know why Anna would set me up with someone as
10   shallow as that! Who dumps a date on her doorstep? He
11   didn't even give me a chance, and if all he wants to base
12   his opinion on is looks — well, he might want to look in
13   a mirror! He's nothing to go crazy over ... I mean, he
14   wasn't bad looking ... but he obviously has no
15   personality! It's a shame, too, because the way Anna
16   talked, we had a lot in common.
17   As of this minute, I'm swearing off blind dates for life.
18   I don't care if I have to sit around every Friday and
19   Saturday night for the rest of my life! I am not going
20   through this torture ...
21   Omigosh! He's back ... he's pulling up to the curb ...
22   what's he want now? To actually puke on me?
23   He's opening his door ... he's getting out ... with
24   flowers ... oh, isn't that sweet? He brought me flowers!
25   And in his other hand ... candy! Maybe that's why he
26   rushed off! He's really very sweet! Oh, this is going to be
27   the best date ever!

19. Flower Girl? At My Age?

(2 girls)

1	*Nicole's Version*
2	NICOLE: This is so humiliating! Not only is my mother trying
3	to ruin my life by getting remarried in the first place —
4	to my assistant principal, I might add — but now she's
5	asking me to be the flower girl. *Hello!* I'm fifteen years
6	old! Doesn't she see how ridiculous it would be to have
7	*me* be the flower girl? Maid of honor, yes. Flower girl, no!
8	She says I'm allowing the "norm" to guide my
9	decision. Well, duh. I *prefer to be normal, Mom!* Just
10	because she's like some hippie flower child who never
11	conforms to the rules of the world doesn't mean that I
12	want to be that way! I *like* fitting in! Being part of a
13	crowd. *Not* standing out like she does. That's who I am!
14	Not a fifteen-year-old flower girl in a wedding that has
15	gone from bizarre to ludicrous!
16	Why couldn't they just slink off and get married? This
17	is her second wedding, after all! Does she really need
18	such a big production? I'm going to be the laughing
19	stock of the school when word gets around that they're
20	not even wearing shoes during the ceremony! How
21	backward is that? It will be bad enough to live down just
22	the wedding stuff — like the no shoes and the tie-dyed
23	tablecloths — but look at me! All puffed out in this
24	ridiculous pink flower girl dress? I don't think so!
25	How am I going to get my nonconformist mother to
26	understand that I cannot be part of this wedding? Isn't it
27	enough that I agreed to attend the stupid thing? Does
28	she really have to humiliate me this way? Can't she see

1   that it's not all about her? This is affecting me, too!
2   There she is. I'm just going to march over there and tell
3   her that I won't do it. I won't. Nothing can make me. Not
4   even guilt. Not even that "you'll break my heart" look she
5   gets on her face ... not even that really cute guy that's
6   standing beside that woman that's standing beside her ...
7   oh, gosh! He saw me! He's coming this way ... what am I
8   gonna do now? He's seen me ... in this fluffy pink thing!
9   He's going to think I'm a geek ... a cotton candy puff ... but
10   he's smiling ... or is he laughing? No ... no, he's smiling. At
11   me. You've got to be kidding! He actually likes this thing?
12   How am I going to change now? He'll think I'm an idiot!
13   Changing before the wedding even starts! I'm stuck! Stuck
14   being the oldest flower girl on the face of the earth! I guess
15   I'll just have to make the most of it!
16
17   *Mother's Version*
18 MOTHER: I know Nicole is upset about being a flower girl in
19   my wedding. I just don't get it either. Who *says* a flower
20   girl has to be a certain age? I want my daughter to be a
21   part of this event and I think it will be adorable for her to
22   toss the flowers before I come in. She's making a big deal
23   out of nothing. Nobody thinks she's a baby for being a
24   flower girl. Everyone can see what a beautiful young lady
25   she is.
26   Why does she worry so much about what everyone
27   expects? Can't she be spontaneous and carefree for just
28   one day? *My day?* It's not too much to ask is it? I swear
29   she took completely after her father. He's so rigid and
30   stiff. Couldn't laugh if he had to unless it was at a boss's
31   joke. He's easily the most unyielding man in the world.
32   No wonder we couldn't stand each other by the time we
33   split up.
34   Oh, we both thought it was cute in the beginning. How
35   different we were. I thought it was sweet how responsible

1   he was. He wanted to take care of me. I never dreamed
2   how controlling he'd become. And I suppose he thought
3   it was wonderful how full of life I was ... at first. Then, I
4   just got on his nerves for not conforming to society. Not
5   wanting to be the no-personality, PTA-president Mom he
6   thought I should be. I was too artsy. He was too formal.
7   I was too loud. He was too quiet. I was too open. He was
8   too closed. We were a mess.
9   So I worry about Nicole being too much like him and
10   not enough like me. How come she can't be a mix of the
11   two of us? Can't she just loosen up a little? Toss her
12   inhibitions to the wind? She looks positively stunning in
13   the pink dress I bought her. I know it's a little much, but
14   why can't she embrace the idea of standing out instead
15   of trying to run and hide from it? This could be her
16   moment to shine and she wants to throw it all away? I'm
17   not trying to turn her into a mini-me. I'm not! I just don't
18   want her becoming a clone of her father! There *is* more
19   to life than business suits and PalmPilots!
20   Maybe one day she'll look back on this day and
21   remember it as the day she threw the flowers to the wind
22   and was set free!

20. Night Owl

(1 guy/1 girl)

Ben's Version

2 BEN: Why is it that I lie awake night after night unable to
3   sleep and yet five minutes into algebra and I'm out like a
4   light?
5   My teacher is ready to suspend me if I fall asleep one
6   more time in her class. You'd think that'd be enough to
7   scare me awake, but no! Even as I sit here, I feel my lids
8   starting to droop. Her voice is so soothing, so c ... a ...
9   l ... m ... i ... n ... g ...
10   *Stop it!* Wake up! Sit up. Look around.
11   OK. There. I'm awake. Maybe she didn't notice my
12   head jerk back.
13   I'm just so tired. ... It's not my fault. I try to go to bed
14   early but I can't sleep. Warm milk. Nothing. Wide awake.
15   I lie there, hour after hour, watching the clock, waiting for
16   morning so I can stop the torture. That's what it is, too.
17   Pure torture! Do you know what kind of weird thoughts a
18   person has at three ... four ... five a.m.? They're not
19   pretty, I can tell you that! I'm starting to think I'm going
20   insane! It's like voices are in my head and I can't turn
21   them off!
22   If only Mrs. Switzer's voice were in my head. That'd
23   put me to sleep for sure! Where is she at two o'clock a.m.
24   when I need her? Why is it now, in a hard uncomfortable
25   chair, that I want to fall asleep?
26   I'm just gonna close my eyes for a second ... she won't
27   even notice ... and they're burning so badly. If I put my
28   book up, she'll never even see me ... just a couple of

1   seconds to refresh me and then I'll be ... f ... i ... n ... e ...
2   zzzzzz ...
3
4   *Teacher's Version*
5   TEACHER: I'm sick and tired of kids who stay up all night
6   and then think they can sleep through my class! I don't
7   know what they're up to at night — partying, surfing the
8   Net, watching movies — whatever! All I know is day after
9   day I have kids like Ben Frost who think I spend my time
10   preparing a lesson so that they can sleep through it!
11   I have to stay up late getting ready for class, grading
12   papers, planning ahead, and I don't get the luxury of a nap
13   during the day, so why should they? Why do they think
14   their time is more important than mine? They might as
15   well skip if they're going to sleep! Either way, I'm going to
16   start suspending them. Especially Ben. He nods off in here
17   at least three times a week. I don't know how he's learning
18   anything and yet he's got an A in this class! He's probably
19   cheating off someone during test time. No one can sleep
20   that much and be learning anything.
21   I see him setting up the scam right now. Trying to
22   slouch down in his chair and prop his book up so he can
23   hide behind it. Does he really think I'm that stupid? Half
24   the time, he even snores! I know the routine. Within five
25   minutes he's going to be out. His head will fall back, and
26   then he'll be mine ... all mine!
27   Sleep, Ben, sleep. I've already got the discipline slip
28   with your name on it. Maybe that'll jerk you awake. I
29   know it will sure make *me* sleep better!

SECTION III
MONOLOGS

That's the Way I See It!

21. The Final Act
(Girl)

1   TAYLOR: I never thought she'd do it. Ever. Not in a million
2   years. Or I would've told someone. Maybe not her
3   parents, especially not her dad, but someone! A teacher,
4   a counselor, my pastor!

5   Now she's dead and it's all my fault. I could've stopped
6   it — stopped her, if I'd just taken her seriously. But
7   Shannon's always been ... overly dramatic. In fact,
8   everyone calls ... called ... her Drama Queen. She even
9   had a sticker on her locker that said it. How was I to
10   know this time it was different?

11   Everything had been going so well for her. She got the
12   lead part in the spring musical, had a date lined up for
13   prom, and a great dress already bought. Bright pink. Her
14   favorite color. Our favorite color.

15   I mean, things were going her way. As usual. Shannon
16   always had things easy. Perfect, really. It's like you just
17   wanted to be near her ... to touch her ...

18   I guess her dad thought so, too. Shannon told me her
19   secret about a month ago. I didn't know whether to
20   believe her at first. I mean, Mr. Hunter was the ultimate
21   father. Always running us places, playing stupid board
22   games, buying special gifts for his daughter. He never
23   missed a game when she cheered. He adored her.

24   I'm still having a hard time convincing myself that it's
25   true. But why else would Shannon have killed herself?
26   Why didn't I tell someone what she'd told me? Even
27   though she swore me to secrecy, I knew better than to
28   keep a secret like that. And then, when she talked about

1   there only being one way out — why didn't I understand
2   what she was implying? Why was I so wrapped up in
3   other things that I couldn't see her changing?

4   Her mother is devastated. Who wouldn't be? She's lost
5   her daughter. No note. No explanation. She's completely
6   dumbfounded as to why Shannon would do this. I can see
7   the self-blaming in her eyes. She thinks she did
8   something wrong.

9   The question is: Do I tell her the secret? Do I take the
10   poor woman's husband (creep that he is!) as well as her
11   child? What if she thinks I'm some sicko, trying to cause
12   trouble?

13   Look at Mr. Hunter, sitting there hunched over, grief-
14   stricken ... or is he guilt-stricken? Does he really think he
15   got away with it? I can't stand to look at him!

16   I'm going to tell Mrs. Hunter. I am. I owe my friend that
17   much. I wasn't there for her before, but I'm going to be
18   now. Shannon, this is for you ...

22. I Was Only Five
(Girl)

1   TARA: I know it wasn't my fault. I mean, a five-year-old
2   should not be left to watch her baby sister, right? My
3   mom should've known that I got distracted easily. Even
4   though she said, "Do not take your eyes off your sister,"
5   she should've known that I would.
6   I remember hearing a familiar song coming from the
7   living room. It was my favorite cartoon! I ran in to watch
8   it. I could hear Mom talking on the phone, arguing with
9   someone, but I blocked it out. I was completely
10   mesmerized by the television.
11   The show was almost over when Mom found me sitting
12   there. "Where's your sister?" she screamed and ran to
13   the bathroom.
14   I didn't even run after her. I remember thinking, *In the*
15   *tub, where else would she be? She can't walk.* So I just
16   sat there. Still watching. Still mesmerized.
17   How could I have known what would happen? I didn't
18   understand about babies slipping down into the water and
19   not coming back up. I didn't know what drowning was.
20   Mom screamed and I heard water splash. "Get the
21   phone! Tara, get me the phone!"
22   Before I could even jump up to get it, Mom came
23   running into the room with Emily in her arms. That's
24   when I knew something was really wrong. She didn't look
25   all pink and rosy like she always did. And she wasn't
26   squirming in Mom's arms and she was always wiggly.
27   That's why we called her "Wiggle Worm." But not now.
28   Now she was limp, her head flopped back over Mom's

1   arm and she had a blue color under her skin.

2   I remember watching the flashing lights move across

3   the walls of our living room and the men that rushed into

4   our house and stayed bent over Emily for a long time.

5   Mom screamed and cried, saying, "It's not my fault. It

6   was an accident. It's not my fault."

7   Even though I was young, I knew what that meant. If

8   it wasn't her fault, then it must've been mine.

9   I've carried around that guilt all of my life. Knowing I

10   left my sister to drown in that tub. I'm old enough now to

11   know it really wasn't my fault. I was too young. Too young

12   to be responsible. But knowing something and believing

13   something are two different things.

14   I'm sorry, Wiggle Worm.

23. Scaredy Cat
(Guy)

1 TYLER: You're gonna think I'm a freak. I'm almost seventeen
2   years old and I still don't have my permit, much less my
3   license. When people find that out, they just look at me
4   like I'm some kind of underachiever — someone too lazy to
5   even study for a simple driving test. Funny thing is, I know
6   that book inside and out. I've read it cover to cover at least
7   ten times. There's not a question they could ask that I
8   wouldn't know. But I guess it's easier to let people believe
9   that I'm stupid or lazy then to tell anyone the truth.
10   See, I'm afraid to drive. Almost every night since I
11   turned sixteen, I've had this nightmare where I'm in a car
12   accident and killed. I see the whole thing — I swerve to
13   avoid a deer, staring at me with these glowing yellow
14   eyes, and then I'm rolling down an embankment. Over
15   and over I roll. Sometimes I wake up screaming, but
16   usually there's just blackness. Total blackness without a
17   single pinpoint of light. Death.
18   OK, so I know the obvious answer. It's just a dream.
19   A stupid nightmare that can't hurt me. But what if it isn't
20   just a stupid nightmare that's haunting me? What if it's
21   more of a premonition and I ignore it? I can't get that out
22   of my head. Every time I even think about going for my
23   test, my hearts starts pounding and my hands get all
24   sweaty and the deer flashes before my eyes. How can I
25   ignore that?
26   My mom thinks I'm not driving so that I don't have to
27   get a job. She looks at me all disappointed like she's
28   raised the world's worst bum of a son. I've told her I'll

1   work — she just has to drive me. But I don't think she

2   wants to be bothered with carting me around.

3   I don't know what to do. I mean, I've got to get my

4   license eventually, right? I can't have my mom drive me

5   around for the rest of my life ... or can I? There isn't a law

6   that says you have to drive, is there? My grandmother

7   never drove a day in her life and she made out OK. Who

8   says that just because I *can* drive, that I *have* to?

9   Of course it will be kind of hard to date that way ...

10   unless ... I date a girl that can drive! Yeah, that'll work!

11   Just think of the money I'll save on gas and insurance!

12   Even car payments! Maybe I'll even get a better bike! One

13   of those road bikes that I can take everywhere ... hey, I'll

14   be saving the environment, too!

24. Gothic
(Girl)

1 CHYNA: I wish everyone would stop staring at me. They
2   stand there all gawking with their mouths hanging open.
3   They don't even try to hide it. They'll be talking and
4   laughing and the minute they see me, everyone stops
5   and stares. They don't even care that I can see them
6   doing it. They nudge each other as I walk by and when
7   my back is to them, their whispering and laughing starts.
8   No one sits by me in class. I guess they think being
9   different is contagious. It's fine with me because I like
10   being alone. I know I don't fit in with them. Who'd want
11   to? They're so afraid to do something that someone
12   won't like. Buy the wrong pants or shirt, or God forbid,
13   wear something without a logo.
14   So what if I like to wear black? It doesn't make me
15   evil. It's not a sin to dress this way. They can dress the
16   way they want, but I can't? It's OK that they have four
17   holes in one ear but I'm a disgusting for having one in my
18   nose? And of course they can tip their black hair blonde
19   but I'm a freak for having green streaks? And just
20   because I wear a studded necklace, I'm a dog? What
21   about them in their look-a-like designer clothes ... does
22   that make them clones?
23   I just don't see why everyone can't be who they want
24   to be. Without being judged. Or condemned.
25   When something bad happens at school, I'm always
26   the first one questioned. The finger is always pointed at
27   me. I've been suspended three times this year already
28   and I haven't done the first thing. I guess it's the price I

1 pay for being different. Daring to stand out from the
2 mindless people surrounding me.
3   So let them whisper and stare and laugh at me. I don't
4 need their approval. I'm fine just the way I am.

25. Baby-Sitting Blues
(Girl)

1   BECKY: I figure I've changed about a thousand diapers since
2   the time I turned eleven. Big family, you ask? No. Becky
3   the Baby-sitter, that's me.
4   I remember how excited I was to take the course at the
5   YWCA. I even made flyers and business cards and
6   passed them out all over the neighborhood. "Becky's
7   Baby-Sitting: Best for Your Baby," I'd say and shove my
8   card in their hand. It took about three weeks before I got
9   my first call and then, wham! I was bombarded.
10   Every weekend I was busy changing diapers, wiping
11   noses, and watching shows on PBS. It was great ... at first.
12   I had more money than I'd ever had in my life. It overflowed
13   my piggy bank and so Mom opened up a savings account
14   for me. I didn't have any trouble saving. I was so busy
15   sitting, I didn't have time to spend any money!
16   It's been that way for five years now. Some of the first
17   kids I ever baby-sat are in kindergarten now. It's so hard
18   to believe.
19   Trouble is, I'm getting tired of the whole thing. I mean,
20   the little snots are really starting to get on my nerves. All
21   that whining and crying. And butt wiping. Yuck! Seems
22   like parents are waiting longer and longer to potty train
23   their kids. Have you ever changed a three-and-a-half-
24   year-old's diaper? It's absolutely disgusting!
25   And parents are more demanding now, too. No more
26   putting in a movie for the kids to watch. Oh no! They
27   want quality time for their little darlings. Finger games.
28   Puppet shows. Crafts. Stories read. I just wonder what

1   the parents do when I'm not around. The kids probably
2   watch television all day and night.
3   And the meals! Mac and cheese used to be my favorite
4   to fix. You can even use those easy packets in the
5   microwave. Quick and hardly any cleanup. But is that
6   good enough for organic, gotta-have-fresh-everything kids
7   today? No! I gotta spend more time in the kitchen than
8   the school cafeteria workers! I should be getting paid
9   double! One fee for sitting and one fee for cooking! Get
10   real! Some parents even want me to do cleaning while
11   I'm there. You know, "If you have time, would you mind
12   straightening up a bit?" Give me a break! I'm the
13   cheapest babysitter/cook/maid you can get! What are
14   people expecting for a lousy three dollars an hour?
15   So as of today, I'm done! Done wiping boogers and
16   butts! I'm getting a real job out in the real world where I
17   don't have to do three jobs for the price of one!
18   Hang on a sec ... *(Pause)* Hello? ... Saturday night? ... I
19   don't think ... overnight? ... Sure, I'll do it! Bye!
20   What can I say? This lady always pays me extra, and
21   overnight means more hours and the little rug rats will be
22   asleep for most of it! You can't beat that!
23   I guess Becky the Baby-sitter can make it one more
24   night! Boogers and butts, here I come!

26. Mom? I Don't Think So
(Girl)

1   LAUREN: It's absolutely ridiculous for my father to expect me
2   to call his wife-to-be "Mom." Besides the obvious fact that
3   I already have a mother, I'm not about to call Miss I'm-
4   Young-Enough-to-Still-Be-Carded "Mom"! When people
5   see us together they think she's my sister! She would've
6   had to have me at eight years old for her to be my mother!
7   How stupid is that? My father is marrying a girl (not a
8   woman!) who wasn't even born when he got married the
9   first time to my mother! That's just sick!
10   I'm not exactly thrilled about the whole stepmother thing
11   as it is, but this is completely embarrassing. People are
12   always staring when we're with my dad because she hangs
13   all over him. It's gross. He looks like a dirty old man.
14   My friends think it's cool to have someone who
15   actually has a clue about clothes and makeup and who
16   actually listens to the same music as I do. I did, too ...
17   at first. We hung out, went shopping, even went to a
18   concert together. Without Dad around it was easy being
19   her friend. But it's weird to see him with her. How can
20   she and I have so much in common and she be marrying
21   my father? Nothing against my dad, but he's old! Yuck!
22   How am I supposed to be expected to think of her as
23   the "mother type"? Have her tell me what to do? I don't
24   think so. It'd be like taking orders from your sister.
25   I just wish Dad would wake up and realize this is never
26   gonna work! He'll be retired and half-dead when she's
27   hitting the prime of her life. Does he really think she'll
28   stay saddled to some old, crumpled up man?

1   Oh, he acts all young now! Taking up tennis! What a
2 joke. He's never played a sport in his life and now he's
3 on the courts every weekend swinging that racket like a
4 lovesick puppy. How long is that gonna last? She'll be
5 pushing him to the courts in a wheelchair! I can see it
6 coming!
7   I even heard him say that he wouldn't mind having a
8 baby with this chick! Doesn't he realize he's old enough
9 to be a grandfather?! And I'm way too old to have a baby
10 brother or sister. I'd take it out for a walk and people
11 would think it's mine! And why wouldn't they? I'm the
12 one getting close to baby age — not my father! He had
13 his chance years ago and he should be happy with the
14 one he got. Besides, he's getting another child by
15 marrying Darla! I'll just die if he marries her!

27. Man of the House
(Guy)

1   DAVID: I don't know who he thinks he is but I can tell you
2   who he's not: my father. Just because my mom married
3   the guy doesn't mean he's anything to me. I've been
4   taking care of things around here ever since my dad died.
5   I even started mowing lawns to help Mom pay the bills.
6   I'm not about to let some bozo waltz in thinking he's
7   going to rule the roost.
8   Mom and I were just fine without him. When she had
9   a problem, she turned to me and vice versa. We were
10   best friends, which isn't even normal 'cause most guys
11   my age only yell and argue with their moms. So why'd
12   she have to go and ruin things? I'll be out of the house
13   soon enough ... couldn't she have waited until then?
14   She's only known this guy for eight months. Isn't that a
15   little fast for running off and tying the knot?
16   And for that matter ... why'd she slink off to do it if
17   she didn't think it was wrong in the first place? She
18   didn't even wait until I could be there! How cold is that?
19   Getting married while your son is at band camp?
20   Of course she probably knew I wouldn't have gone
21   anyway. How could I stand there and watch her make the
22   biggest mistake of her life? There's no way I could've
23   kept my mouth shut at that "does anybody object" part,
24   that's for sure!
25   It's not that I don't want my mom to be happy ... I
26   do ... but ... we were! Friday nights were always the best!
27   That was our movie night. We'd watch two or three
28   movies and pig out on popcorn and chocolate. Now she

1   wants me to do that with her and her new hubby? I don't
2   think so. I'm not gonna be a third wheel. The guy's
3   probably hoping to ship me off to military school or
4   something. I'm sure I'm in the way ... well, he can forget
5   about coming in and taking over. I'm man of the house.
6   Not him. I just wish Dad were here. Then we'd show the
7   guy who's boss.

28. Epitaph?

(Guy)

1 DONALD: This is so weird! I just heard people ramble on and
2 on about how wonderful my father was and all I can think
3 is, *Am I at the wrong funeral?* Who in the heck were they
4 talking about?
5 A giving man. A kind man. Someone you could turn
6 to. A real friend. What?!
7 My dad? *My* dad? How could he have been so nice ...
8 so different to all these people and so hateful to me?
9 There has to be some logical explanation. Maybe they're
10 just saying those things to be nice. Lying because no one
11 would ever say something bad about a dead man.
12 Especially at his funeral ... in front of his family ... but
13 don't they think we know how horrible he was?
14 Or was he? Could he have been different to them? I
15 just don't get it!
16 I sat there listening. Trying hard to believe what they
17 said. Trying to see a glimpse of that person they
18 described. Where had he been all my life? This man that
19 everyone else seemed to like. How was it that virtual
20 strangers had better memories of my father than me?
21 How could he have given them the best and saved the
22 worst for us?
23 How am I supposed to smile politely when I really want
24 to shout out and call them liars! Make them admit that
25 he was nothing like what they're saying! I'm having a
26 hard time even looking like I'm mourning. Now my mind
27 is so jumbled with these things they've said that I don't
28 even know what to think. Was it just me all these years?

1   Did he only treat my badly? What did I do to deserve
2   that?
3   I try to remember the good times, though very few and
4   far between. But the bad always out-shadows those brief
5   moments and all I can think of is how mean he was. Does
6   that make me a bad person? My dad is dead and I can't
7   remember one nice thing about him!
8   Truth is, part of me is even glad that he died ... surely
9   that makes me even worse than he ever was! But how
10   can I just pretend he was someone he wasn't? How can
11   I forgive him when he never said he was sorry ... not once
12   for anything he ever did ... he never even said he loved
13   me. ...
14   I'm sorry ... but this man they are talking about ... I
15   never knew him.

29. A Coupon?
(Girl)

1 PAULA: Sometimes I can't believe what I put up with. I bust
2 my butt rushing around making sure everybody gets their
3 food hot and that their drinks are full and this is how they
4 thank me? A lousy coupon for buy-one-get-one-free pizza?
5 This is easily the worst tip I've ever gotten. I can't even eat
6 pizza! I'm lactose intolerant and the cheese tears up my
7 stomach! I just can't believe how ungrateful people are. I
8 swear I've actually had a man snap his fingers at me ...
9 like I'm some kind of dog he can call back to the table! I
10 guess waitress means slave to some people. Don't they
11 see I've got other customers? I can only do so much ...
12   Sometimes I'd like to just "accidentally" trip with a
13 tray of food right into an annoying customer's lap. Like
14 Mr. Finger Snap. I'd love to see his expression as food
15 was flying his way! A Kodak moment for sure!
16   What gets me most are tightwads. They'll spend a
17 hundred dollars on drinks and dinner and then when it's
18 time for the tip, they figure *exactly* fifteen percent on a
19 napkin. Not leaving a penny more than they should. I
20 know I should be grateful they leave that — most people
21 don't even come close to that!
22   There's this one family that comes in every Sunday
23 (probably after church) and their bill is always at least
24 forty dollars. What do they leave me? Two dollars. Two
25 dollars for bringing two adults and two kids their food and
26 drinks. That's a whopping fifty cents apiece! Wow! I'll
27 take that to the bank right away! Get a clue people! Even
28 ten percent would be four dollars!

1   It's not rocket science to figure out a tip. Why don't
2   customers take out one of their precious cell phones and
3   use the calculator every now and then? They sure don't
4   mind taking it out to talk — in the middle of ordering!
5   Like I've got nothing better to do than stand there and let
6   them finish their conversation! There I am, pen in air,
7   looking like an idiot while they're chatting away.
8   And let me tell you a thing about most parents — they
9   think I live to clean up after their kid! Little Johnny boy
10   will crush about ten packages of crackers and dump
11   them on the floor with his half-eaten chicken fingers and
12   fries and does anyone bother to scoop some of it up?
13   Heck no. The waitress will do that. It's her job. She lives
14   to serve. I wonder what their houses look like since
15   apparently most kids eat like pigs!
16   I haven't even gotten to the *best* part about waitressing —
17   the dirty old men who try to grab my rear end! Don't they
18   know they're in a restaurant and not a strip club? I have
19   friends that actually encourage it because they know
20   they'll get better tips that way. Not me. I'm there to serve
21   food ... not my body. Catcalls, snapping fingers, lousy
22   tips ... it almost makes it understandable when you hear
23   about servers spitting in food ... not that I've ever done
24   that ... but I've sure been tempted.
25   Oh, look! It's the fifty-cent family ... and they brought
26   friends ... maybe today I'll make a whole *dollar* for the
27   hour and a half that they think they own me!

30. Third Time Is Not the Charm
(Guy)

1   ADAM: I guess I saw it coming. I just didn't want to believe it.
2   I mean, geesh, it's her third husband already, you'd think
3   one of these times she'd learn how to make it stick. Not
4   that I'm blaming it all on my mother — God knows she
5   picks some real winners. And I'm not exactly torn up about
6   seeing this one go, but the timing sure was kind of lousy.
7   Here I come, bags in hand from football camp, and
8   there she is waiting on the porch. For a split second I
9   thought maybe she'd missed me, was actually waiting
10   there to greet me. I should've known better. She was
11   there to break the news: Gary moved out while I was
12   gone, and with him — half our house. She wanted to tell
13   me before I walked in and saw that the good television
14   and almost all of the living room furniture was missing.
15   Seems like every time we get something halfway decent
16   Mom marries another guy who somehow ends up taking
17   it when he leaves. I haven't figured that one out exactly.
18   I guess it's the payoff for getting them out, I don't know.
19   Now she's all teary-eyed and hysterical. I'm supposed
20   to comfort her and tell her everything is going to be OK.
21   I know the routine. She'll swear off dating for about a
22   week, if that, and then she'll be back out at the bars
23   trying to meet the next Mr. Right. After that, it's never
24   long before someone else is moving his things into our
25   house. No ring. No promises. Just stuff. After awhile
26   Mom will start pressing for marriage and before I know it,
27   she's got some cheap gold wedding band on her finger
28   and she's announcing I've got a new stepdad. Problem is,

1   none of these guys have ever cared a hoot about me. She
2   doesn't exactly pick the fatherly type. And then she
3   wonders why they end up being drunks or losers that quit
4   their jobs and live off her.
5   You'd think by now the guys would see that there's
6   only one kind of door on this house: a revolving one.
7   Mom's jealous rages and extreme highs and lows usually
8   run them off before too long. I'm always surprised at how
9   well she hides that side of her until she gets that ring on
10 her finger.
11   I almost feel sorry for the poor unsuspecting guys who
12 fall prey to her trap. I even tried warning this last one but
13 he just thought I was some punk kid who didn't want
14 another man in the house. I guess he thinks differently
15 now, but I'll never know. Once their stuff is gone, I never
16 see them again. Can't wait until it's my turn to get out. I
17 just wonder what furniture I'll get to take.

31. Have a Slice
(Girl)

 1 CHARLOTTE: It certainly wasn't the smartest thing I've ever
 2   done, I'll admit to that, but I know people who do far
 3   worse things. Sometimes you can't see the forest for the
 4   trees, right? You get so focused on what you're doing, you
 5   forget to stop and think things through.
 6   That's what happened to me. See, I had this piece of
 7   candy and my friend Millie wanted part of it. No problem
 8   if it's gum or taffy, but of course that's not what I had. I
 9   had a small square fruit chew that really shouldn't even
10   be called a "chew" because you pretty much have to
11   suck on the thing for a long time before it's ever soft
12   enough to chew. Anyhow, obviously it was too hard to
13   break with my hands. Now any other person would've
14   probably just given it to the person. Oh no. Not me. We
15   were gonna *share* that stinking thing.
16   I remembered I had this cool little pocketknife in my
17   purse. I don't think I'd ever even used the knife part
18   before, just the nail file. Anyway, it seemed perfectly
19   logical to cut the candy in half, right? My boyfriend,
20   Frank, who was driving the car, and Millie, who was in
21   the back seat, sure didn't speak up and say anything
22   when I started sawing away. So I guess you could say
23   they're not any smarter than me.
24   Anyhow, I think it would've worked OK had I been
25   patient, except the sawing wasn't making much of a dent.
26   I decided to push hard and slice through the candy instead.
27   *Bingo!* Not only did it cut the candy in half, almost
28   perfectly I might add, but it sliced right through my

1 finger! Blood started gushing everywhere! I screamed,
2 Millie screamed, and Frank screamed. Only he was
3 yelling at me to stick my hand out the window because
4 he didn't want blood all over his car ... you gotta love
5 guys, don't you?
6   So there I was, my arm out the window with him flying
7 down the road and blood spewing all over the side of the car.
8   There was so much blood. I started to think I'd cut the
9 end of my finger off, only I was too afraid to look down at
10 my lap to see if my finger was lying there. Everything
11 started to whirl before my eyes and I told Frank and Millie
12 that I was going to pass out. "Put your head down!"
13 Frank told me and he shoved my head between my
14 knees. He drove straight to the hospital.
15   The lady at the desk looked at me like I was an idiot.
16 I guess I can't blame her; they must get a lot of weird
17 people in the emergency room. But I wanted to yell out,
18 "I'm not stupid! I swear! I'm a straight-A student! I don't
19 normally do dumb things like this!"
20   But as I was sitting there covered in blood, holding a
21 rag over my throbbing finger, I was pretty sure that no
22 one would believe me.

32. Curfew
(Girl)

1   ASHLEY: I don't understand why I have to have a stupid
2   curfew. My parents say they trust me — well, apparently
3   they don't, because they think I need all these rules to
4   stay out of trouble. I feel like a baby when I have to tell
5   my friends that I have to leave — just when a party
6   starts kicking. Almost everyone else stays out past
7   midnight and here I am stuck with an eleven o'clock
8   curfew. I can't even go to the nine o'clock movie and get
9   home on time! I'm stuck at the seven o'clock showing
10   with all the little kids and old people!
11   I've never been in trouble in my life! So why can't my
12   parents cut me a little slack? Obviously I've got good
13   judgment. If I want to stay out later, I think I should be
14   able to decide. I don't need them controlling my life and
15   making all my decisions. Next year I'll be off to college.
16   What're they gonna do then? Follow me and make sure
17   I'm in my room on time?
18   It's like they think if they gave me a little leeway, I'll
19   go wild or something. Don't they even know me? I'm
20   president of Students Against Drunk Driving at school,
21   doesn't that say something? Do they really think I'm
22   going to act irresponsibly? What do I have to do to prove
23   to them that I can be trusted?
24   Besides, I work. I pay my own insurance and gas. Why
25   should I have to listen to them? It's my car! If I want to
26   stay out driving around all night I should be able to! I
27   think tonight I'm just gonna come home whenever I
28   want. I'm old enough to make my own choices and it's

1   high time they saw that. They need to wake up and
2   accept the fact that I'm growing up and need to be
3   treated that way.
4   I have friends that just lie about where they're going
5   or where they've been, using sleepovers as excuses to
6   stay out all night. My parents should be grateful that I tell
7   them the truth. And the truth today is: Mom and Dad,
8   don't wait up. I'm gonna be late!

33. Sister Envy
(Guy)

1   ETHAN: I am so sick of my sister getting everything she wants.
2   All she has to do is start crying and Dad caves in like a
3   bad mudslide. You know what she got on her sixteenth
4   birthday? A brand new car! And not just any old car but
5   a shiny red convertible Corvette! Now who buys one of
6   those for a sixteen-year-old? My parents, obviously!
7   But here's the real kicker! Know what I got on my
8   sixteenth birthday? A ten-year-old pickup truck with as
9   many cigarette burns in the upholstery as rust spots in
10   the paint! The exhaust comes out as thick gray smoke,
11   and half the time it dies whenever I hit the brakes! It's a
12   real winner, I tell you! Want to know what my dad said
13   when I asked where *my* Corvette was? "Oh, we could
14   never afford the insurance on one of those for you! Boys
15   are so much harder to insure!"
16   So she gets a sports car and I get a piece of junk?
17   That's how it's been all my life. Daddy's little angel gets
18   absolutely everything she could possibly want. She never
19   even has to lift a finger around here. I take out the
20   garbage. I mow the lawn. I have to vacuum. I even
21   empty the dishwasher! I do everything while she sits
22   around like a princess talking on the phone and painting
23   her nails! And my parents wonder why the two of us
24   don't get along!
25   Why can't they see how unfair it is around here? I don't
26   want a lot — just a little equality! Isn't there an
27   amendment to protect me or something? I'm sick of her
28   getting off scot-free!

1   What'd I ever do to be treated this way? Being born a
2   boy — that's what! I wish I lived in China — now they've
3   got the right idea! Didn't they kill off all the girls or
4   something like that? Boy babies are revered! And that's
5   the way it should be! That'd be a real change around here,
6   I can tell you that! I'd love to see her doing chores every
7   day while I'm riding around town with the top down and the
8   wind blowing *my* hair! She wouldn't feel so puffed up riding
9   in my beat up old truck, now would she? Yeah ... that'd be
10   the perfect life ...

34. Bambi Killer

(Guy)

1　TED:　I swear if I get called Bambi Killer one more time I may
2　　　　just go postal! What is it with people? They living in
3　　　　Disney World or what? Get a clue people! Deer *do not*
4　　　　talk! And their little friends don't either!
5　　　　　Just because I'm a hunter does not mean I'm on a
6　　　　rampage killing all the cute little fuzzy deer! Doesn't
7　　　　anyone understand the concept of *overpopulation?* As a
8　　　　hunter, I'm helping preserve the species, not just
9　　　　walking around needlessly shooting things that move!
10　　　I'm tired of people making me feel like a low-life
11　　　murderer! Do they feel bad for squashing spiders or
12　　　hacking snakes to bits?
13　　　　Hunting is a skillful sport, like any other. We're not
14　　　just a bunch of killing machines walking around with
15　　　guns and a vengeance against cute furry forest animals!
16　　　I bet everybody would be shocked to know that I've got
17　　　pet rabbits at home. They think that because I'm a
18　　　hunter I hate animals. That's so ignorant! I've got four
19　　　dogs and a cat, too. I am not anti-animals!
20　　　　The same idiots that look down their noses at hunters
21　　　have no problem eating a hamburger or a piece of fried
22　　　chicken! What hypocrites! Where do they think dinner
23　　　comes from?
24　　　　I feel like everyone's just waiting for me to go ballistic
25　　　or something, just because I own a gun. In this day and
26　　　age, I understand being a little paranoid, but just
27　　　because I wear camouflage pants doesn't mean I think
28　　　I'm fighting some kind of war or something! Why can't

1   everyone understand that hunters are not the dredges of
2   society — we don't need everyone looking down at us ...
3   fearing us ... despising us.
4   I guarantee the minute you hit a deer with your car and
5   total it, you'll be wishing a hunter had been around
6   weeding out the population a little. If we didn't hunt, deer
7   would run rampant, and in the winter they'd starve. Yeah,
8   that's better, isn't it? Letting the beautiful creatures die
9   a slow torturous death of starvation rather than being
10   killed instantly and humanely.
11   I should be thanked instead of condemned. I'm proud
12   of every deer I've ever killed. It means other babies and
13   mothers can live. I am a hunter and proud of it.

35. Freak Show
(Guy)

1   MATTHEW: I'm a freak. Just look at me. What? Can't see what
2   the big deal is? Look harder. Come on. Here. I'll give you
3   a little hint. *(Hold up foot.)* See this? Size ten. See this?
4   *(Hold up other foot.)* Size eleven. A whole size difference.
5   Not just a measly little half size! I'm a freak of nature.
6   An experiment gone wrong. Like Dr. Frankenstein
7   couldn't find two feet the same size when he put me
8   together!
9   Do you know how hard it is to buy shoes with these
10 feet? I have to sneak a shoe out of each box and pray that
11 they don't check the sizes at the counter. I can't tell you
12 how many times I've heard, "Oh, wait. You've got two
13 different sizes here. Did you want the tens or the
14 elevens?" Then I stand there like an idiot while they go
15 get me one size or the other.
16   Sometimes I just bolt out the door and then cross that
17 place off my list to shop. Other times I have to buy the
18 stupid shoes, and then have someone return them for me
19 later. I guess the right thing to do would be to buy both
20 pairs, right? But who the heck can afford that? I can
21 barely buy the sneakers I want as it is! I sure can't afford
22 two pairs just so I can throw one shoe from each away!
23   Besides the fact that I'm a shoe-buying nightmare,
24 having two different sized feet makes walking a
25 challenge. I'm constantly tripping over my own feet and
26 then acting like there's something on the floor. "What?
27 You didn't *see* that speck of dirt jump up and trip me?"
28 It could just as well be that I'm an uncoordinated

1   buffoon, but if you had freaky feet, wouldn't you blame
2   them, too?

3   You're probably thinking it's no big deal. That I'm
4   making way too much of it. I mean, people have big
5   noses, big heads, big teeth ... what's so bad about one
6   big foot? Well, that's just it! I only have one! If I had two
7   of the same size I could actually deal with it. I mean, if
8   people had *two* big noses, I think they'd be a little upset,
9   don't you?

10   Anyway, I had it all worked out. I was going to join the
11   circus. Wanna know what they said? I'm not freakish
12   enough! *Not freakish enough!* What a joke! Just look at
13   these things! So here I am stuck in the "normal" world
14   sneaking shoes into boxes and hoping for clueless clerks!

36. Pet Killer
(Guy)

1   CODY: I am easily the lowest person on earth. Really. Lower
2   than the sleaziest, grossest person you can think of.
3   Lower than the pond scum or the thing that eats the
4   pond scum. See, not only did I kill my sister's dog, I lied
5   about it!
6   It all happened yesterday after school. I'd forgotten my
7   uniform for work so I had to run home to get it. I was just
8   going to rush in, grab it off my floor, and then zoom off
9   to work. I'd change in the bathroom once I got there to
10   save time. Obviously, I was focused on getting to work as
11   quickly as possible.
12   That's why I didn't see Rex behind the car. I didn't
13   even realize the thud was him until I was all the way out
14   in the street and saw him lying on the sidewalk. I could
15   tell immediately that he wasn't going to get up. Ever.
16   I'm not a total jerk — I did take the time to make sure
17   that he was dead. I jumped out and ran over to him. No
18   doubt about it. He had guts oozing out of his side and he
19   wasn't breathing. I felt horrible. Even though he was
20   technically my sister's dog, we all loved him. Half the time
21   he slept in *my* bed instead of hers. He was a great dog.
22   I wanted to stay and explain ... be there when Cindy
23   got home from school ... so I could be the one to tell
24   her ... but I was so close to being late and one more
25   tardy at work meant I'd be fired. And fired of course
26   meant no paycheck and no paycheck meant no car. Now
27   I know how horrible that sounds — how cruel and cold
28   you must think I am — but the fact was, the dog was

1   dead and there was nothing I could do about it. Me being
2   late to work would just add to the tragedy, right?
3   Of course Cindy was still sobbing when I got home
4   from work later, and here's where the lying came in. I
5   figured out real quick that no one knew it was me that hit
6   and killed Rex. Cindy kept saying, "Who would do such a
7   thing and just drive off? Leave him lying there like that?
8   Who could do something like that?"
9   How could I possibly tell her it was me? I felt bad
10   enough and she did, too. Would knowing I was the one
11   who killed Rex make things any better? No. So I didn't
12   tell her.
13   Now I feel dirty and ashamed. No job is worth the guilt
14   I feel. I want to tell Cindy the truth. Really. But to be
15   honest, nothing can bring Rex back and the truth would
16   only hurt her more. I guess the price I'll pay is living with
17   this for the rest of my life.
18   Somehow I'll make it up to her.

37. They Expect Me to Live Here?
(Girl)

1 LESLEY: Do we still live in the Dark Ages or what? A
2 concrete floor? You've got to be kidding me! I thought it
3 was a joke at first. That maybe the carpet was being
4 replaced or getting cleaned or something. But when I
5 asked the woman showing me around, she looked at me
6 like I was crazy! *They* have concrete floors and *I'm* crazy?
7 If this was their idea of "wining and dining" me to get me
8 to pick their university, then they must think they're
9 getting students from the bottom of the grade barrel!

10 I'm a straight-A student! I'm not going to live in some
11 decrepit dormitory for four years! Oh, and get this! The
12 *walls* were concrete, too! Painted some lame version of
13 yellow! It looked like a prison cell, not a room. They expect
14 people to *pay* for that! It's complete robbery! I could live
15 *off* campus, but of course they won't allow freshman to do
16 that! Who else could they get to *live* like this?

17 The showers are community showers! How completely
18 gross is that? I know how disgusting my sisters can be,
19 leaving globs of toothpaste in the sink and hair in the
20 drain! This will be a million times worse than that!
21 Twenty girls sharing a bathroom? I don't think so! And
22 get this, I have to walk all the way down the hall every
23 time I need to go to the bathroom! Even in the middle of
24 the night!

25 How can they call these accommodations? All the
26 room has is a bed, a dresser, and a desk. Make that *two*
27 beds! They actually expect people to cram a roommate
28 in that little prison cell. Yeah, right. My bathroom at

1 home is bigger than that! Where am I going to put all my

2 stuff? I can't fit half my things in there!

3   Well, this college is definitely off my list! Concrete

4 floors, community bathrooms! I'm no princess, but I'm

5 not a convict either! All I've got to say is this: If they want

6 me to go to their college, they'd better come up with

7 some better accommodations!

38. Seventeen at Last!
(Guy)

1 CLAYTON: This is it! I'm finally seventeen! Finally able to waltz
2   up to the counter, ID in hand, and buy whatever movie
3   ticket I want. Finally get to see the forbidden R-rated fruit
4   that's been taunting me for all these years! I've got friends
5   whose parents have bought their tickets for them since
6   they were fourteen! But not mine! Oh no. They think the
7   rating is like a *law,* not a suggestion! They won't even rent
8   an R-rated movie for me! Do you know how embarrassing
9   that is?
10   So here I go, on my own, whether my parents like it or
11   not, to view my first R-rated movie. I've even got popcorn
12   and a large drink. This is going to be so awesome! *(Turn*
13   *around, pause, then turn back to audience.)*
14   I think I'm going to vomit! I've never seen so much
15   blood and guts in all my life! I swear they really killed
16   somebody because that stuff looked so real! How do they
17   get it to look that way? So real! Why would anyone want
18   to see that? What kind of sickos make these movies? One
19   guy's head was blown completely off his body. I really
20   think I'm gonna hurl! Is all that blood really necessary? I
21   mean, I think we can get the point without being totally
22   grossed out. One butcher scene was plenty ... did it really
23   have to go on and on like that?
24   If this is what R-rated movies are all about then maybe
25   I haven't been missing out like I thought. Right now, I
26   wouldn't care if I ever saw another human body being
27   blown and splattered across the screen again!
28   Maybe the people who rate these movies need to think

1	a little harder. Do seventeen-year-olds really need to see
2	stuff like that?
3	For that matter ... does anyone?
4	Maybe they need a new rating: GL for *gore lovers!* Then
5	we'd see what kind of sickos really go to these kinds of
6	movies ... and stay far, far away from them! They're sick,
7	after all!

39. Blowout
(Girl)

1   TANYA: I can never go to school again. Never. I'm totally
2   serious. I cannot step foot in school! I am so
3   embarrassed. Everyone will be talking about this for the
4   rest of the year. Maybe even the rest of my life! I can see
5   it now. I'll be voted "Most Dynamic Person." Dynamic
6   meaning dynamite, of course! After today's explosion, I'll
7   never live the wisecracks down.

8   I just can't believe it happened! How could it slip out
9   like that without any warning? There I was in gym when
10   I noticed my shoe was untied. No big deal, right? Wrong.
11   I bent over and when I did, everything broke loose! Out
12   of my pants! It sounded worse than anything even my
13   father or brother can muster up!

14   Of course the gym is usually so loud you couldn't hear
15   a real bomb explode. But no! Not right then! I had
16   the extreme bad fortune of bending over at the exact
17   same time that Mr. Gibson blew the whistle to hold all
18   the basketballs and get quiet. And for some inexplicable
19   reason, everyone actually did. You could've heard a pin
20   drop — it was *that* quiet! Until I let loose, that is. That
21   sound reverberated around the room like a cannon shot.

22   I didn't want to stand back up. I wanted to melt into the
23   floor like the wicked witch in *The Wizard of Oz*. The whole
24   class was laughing. I'm pretty sure Mr. Gibson was, too,
25   but there was no way I was looking up to find out for sure.

26   As quickly as I could, I finished tying my shoe and
27   then bolted to the locker room. I hid out in the stall until
28   the very last moment of class. I tried not to listen to the

1   girls whispering in the dressing room. I knew they were
2   talking about me.
3   Walking down the hall to the next class, I swear
4   everyone knew. It was like the parting of the Red Sea
5   wherever I walked. They must've announced it on the
6   loudspeaker while I was hiding out! I couldn't look anyone
7   in the eye.
8   It's so unfair! Why is it that a guy can do it and
9   everyone gives him a high five but a girl does it and she's
10 like a leper?
11 Anyway, now you can see why I'll have to be
12 homeschooled for the rest of high school. Who cares if I
13 miss my senior year ... and senior prom ... it's no big
14 deal, right?
15 I can tell you one thing: I'll never eat a bean and
16 cheese burrito for lunch ever again!

40. One Time Only
(Girl)

1   CRYSTAL: I know everybody thinks that Mike is a sleazeball.
2   No one wants me to date him. But they just don't
3   understand him like I do. Sure, he's got a temper, but
4   who doesn't? And he only hit me that one time ... well,
5   twice if you count that time he pushed me into the
6   lockers, but that was no big deal. Everyone snaps now
7   and then, right? And I did make things worse because I
8   could tell he was getting really angry and I just kept
9   going on and on. I should've just shut up, you know?
10   So he hit me. Not as hard as he could have, that's for
11   sure. That's gotta be worth something, right? I mean, if
12   he'd wanted to he could've knocked me flat to the floor.
13   I've seen him do it before. He tried to control it this time
14   and I could tell he was just as surprised as I was when
15   he did it. He's really sorry now. He's apologized a million
16   times and he swears he'll never hit me again. I know I
17   can trust him. He loves me. Besides, he really is sorry.
18   And it was mostly my fault, after all. Even he said so.
19   Said I pushed him past his limit. Everybody has a limit,
20   right? And I never know when to stop. Just ask my mom.
21   She says I push, push, push until I get my way or until
22   the other person snaps. It's not like Mike's the first
23   person to ever hit me.
24   Maybe now I'll learn to keep my mouth shut. I sure don't
25   want to go through that again. The look on Mike's face
26   was really scary. I'd never seen him look like that before.
27   So angry. I guess he got that from his dad. He used to
28   beat up on Mike before he took off and left him. So I can't

1   blame Mike, because that's all he knows. Anyway, we can
2   work this out. He's not a bad guy ... really ... it was only
3   once ... I'm sure he won't do it again ...
4   Well, I'm pretty sure ...

41. Talentless

(Girl)

1 ERICA: Who ever heard of a *mandatory* talent show? That's
2   got to be against some sort of right I have, doesn't it?
3   The right to not be totally embarrassed in front of the
4   whole class? I have *no* talent. I'm serious. What am I
5   supposed to do up there? Breathe well?
6   I can't sing, can't dance, baton twirl, eat fire, pull a
7   rabbit out of my hat, play an instrument — nothing! I'm
8   completely talentless. If that's even a word. See, I don't
9   even know if words are real or not! How can I be forced
10   to perform — for a grade — when I don't have anything I
11   can do?
12   So think, Erica, think. What lame thing can I do?
13   Well, I read well. I could bore the class by reading a
14   chapter of a book or something — now that'd go over
15   well, wouldn't it? I wonder if I'd get extra credit for
16   putting the class to sleep?
17   I can just picture all the cheerleaders doing a joint
18   talent — some cute little cheer or dance number where
19   their butts are hanging out of their skirts and the guys
20   are drooling all over the place. Mr. Stephens will give
21   them an A for sure! How am I supposed to compete with
22   that? Pretend I can belly dance or maybe do some kind
23   of strip tease? I wonder if Mr. Stevens would install a
24   pole so I can pole dance ... ha, ha.
25   It's just not fair. I know he thinks we've all got some
26   kind of hidden talent, but he's wrong! If I've got one, it's
27   hidden so far down it's never coming up! And it's
28   certainly not going to sprout up in front of the class.

1   Maybe I'll just be sick tomorrow ... and the rest of the
2   week. By the time I get back, he'll have moved on to
3   some other lame assignment.
4   That's it! I'll be off the hook. Better yet, I'll tell him my
5   great aunt or somebody died. I'll even cry. He'll have to
6   feel sorry for me then! Hey! Maybe I do have a talent ... a
7   talent for lying well and avoiding utter embarrassment!

42. Needy
(Guy)

1   KYLE: My girlfriend, Mackenzie, is *so* needy! Talk about high
2   maintenance! She wants to celebrate absolutely every
3   moment of every part of our relationship! One month
4   anniversary, two month anniversary, and so on ...
5   anniversary of first date, anniversary of first kiss! I'm
6   serious! And in between those you've got all the regular
7   holidays — Thanksgiving, Christmas, Valentine's Day,
8   Sweetheart's Day ... now what's up with that? Isn't
9   Sweetheart's Day the same thing as Valentine's Day?
10 Who made that one up? A girl, no doubt!
11   I'm so busy buying gifts and writing cute little love
12 notes to go with them, I'm about to go crazy! And broke!
13 Not to mention I'm running out of ideas. How can anyone
14 possibly make every other day special? Can't we have
15 just one, plain ordinary moment?
16   If I forget one memorable occasion, she gets all teary-
17 eyed and says I don't care about her. That I'm taking her
18 for granted. What about *her* taking *me* for granted? Where
19 is it written that *I'm* the one who has to buy all the
20 flowers, candy, jewelry, and stuff? When is she gonna
21 fork over some cash on me? She gets away with writing
22 "love" poems or giving me a picture — of herself! How is
23 that fair?
24   I can just hear you now — so break up with her. And
25 I've thought about it. Really. My wallet can't take much
26 more. But every time I try, she looks at me with those
27 beautiful blue eyes and I can't find the words to do it.
28 Then we'll kiss and once we lock lips, it's all over.

1   Sometimes she's really thoughtful, too. Like when I was
2   sick one time and she made me homemade chicken
3   noodle soup. Sure, it didn't taste all that great, but at
4   least she made the effort! I mean, I can't ask for more
5   than that, can I? So what if she's a little sentimental
6   about every time we've ever done anything ... that's just
7   sweet ... right? I should be grateful that those things
8   mean so much to her ... I'm just being a heel for even
9   complaining.
10   Well, I gotta run. Tomorrow's the anniversary of the
11   first time I ate dinner at her house and I've got to get a
12   present!

43. What Did I Do?

(Girl)

1   ELIZABETH: This is such a crock. *My* parents decide they
2   want a divorce and now *I'm* the one stuck in a counseling
3   session? They're the ones with the problems, not *me!* Why
4   do I have to sit here, spilling my guts and talking about my
5   "feelings" if they're the ones bailing out of their marriage?
6   Shouldn't they be the ones talking to a shrink? They didn't
7   even ask me if I needed or wanted to talk to someone.
8   Just made the appointment like that gets them off the
9   hook for what they're putting me through. They have some
10   stranger talk to me so they don't have to!
11   Well, they can make me go but they can't make me
12   talk! I don't have to tell this "couldn't be a real doctor"
13   anything. Although if I wanted to, I could tell her plenty!
14   Like how my "loving" parents have been using me as a
15   go-between in their nasty little battles since the time I
16   could talk! Or how they both talk about each other like
17   dogs to me. How they constantly make me feel like I have
18   to choose one over the other!
19   Yeah, they'd be pretty upset if I actually opened up and
20   told this woman all the horrible things they've done. How
21   about that time Mom hit Dad with a frying pan and he
22   had to get stitches in his head? Or the time Dad locked
23   Mom out of the house and she had to get the police to
24   force him to let her in? Of course there's always that *fun*
25   family vacation we had where they both got mad and left
26   the hotel for over five hours! No big deal, right? Except
27   that I was only seven years old at the time! Hardly old
28   enough to be left alone!

1	See, I've got plenty of dirt on them and I could really
2	let loose ... if I wanted to ... I just don't see the point.
3	How is my venting to some lady with a yellow pad of
4	paper going to make things better? My parents are still
5	going to harass each other — through me, of course, and
6	they're still going to end up divorced.
7	To be honest, that may not be such a bad thing. I'm
8	tired of it all. Being in the middle. Having to choose.
9	Holding all of this in ... the years of their fighting and
10	completely forgetting that I have ears and can *hear*
11	*everything they say.* But why let it out now? They're
12	getting divorced ... it's over ... I can move on ...
13	*(Pause)* What? You want me to scream? Right now?
14	Here in this office ... as loud as I want? ... You're sure?
15	OK. Here goes. *(Scream.)*
16	Wow. You're right. That feels kind of good. I like that.
17	You know, sometimes I feel like screaming ...

44. Random Violence
(Guy)

1　LINCOLN: There I was. Minding my own business. Backpack
2　on, waiting to cross the street, thinking of the calculus
3　test I should've studied more for, when, *wham!* Out of
4　nowhere a fist connects with my jaw, my glasses are
5　knocked off, and I'm flying backward. I don't even
6　attempt to get back up at first. I just sit there stunned,
7　not understanding who or what just hit me. I hear feet
8　pounding the pavement as my assailant runs off to join
9　his friends. I know it's a "he" now because I hear his
10　voice as he's running, "Did you see that?" he yells. "One
11　little punch and the guy hit the ground."
12　　I grope around for my glasses and find them half-under
13　one of my legs. Mangled, but the lenses still good.
14　Holding them up to one eye, I see the group of kids
15　running off. None of them look familiar. Who were they
16　and what did they want? Not money, obviously, since
17　both my backpack and wallet are still with me. Why had
18　they lashed out at me? What had I done to any of them?
19　　The left side of my face is pounding, but I can still
20　move my jaw. A good sign. And though there's some
21　blood, there's not a lot. Very clinically, as if I'm assessing
22　someone else, I think that it could've been worse. I try to
23　push myself off the ground but can't help screaming out
24　in pain. Apparently I'd landed on my hand, and judging
25　from the sharp needlelike feeling shooting up my arm, I'd
26　broken it.
27　　I hold my hand against me while I stand. My legs are
28　shaking. Everything is blurry. Someone calls out to me,

1   "Hey! Are you OK?" And I nod, even though I'm not. The
2   clinical assessment dissolves into full-fledged panic. I
3   want to cry but don't, wishing that it'd been anything but
4   my hand.
5   See, I'm an artist. A real good one, too. Everyone
6   thinks I'll get a full ride to college. That's why winning at
7   State is important. That's why I hadn't studied for
8   calculus like I should have. I was painting. Trying to finish
9   the piece I would submit for the contest. Now I knew it
10   would never get done in time. Hands take a long time to
11   heal. Longer than I had to wait.
12   That's when it hit me. I *had* been robbed. Robbed of
13   the freedom to walk down the street unafraid. Robbed of
14   the innocence that if you mind your own business, people
15   will leave you alone. But mostly, robbed of my one and
16   only chance to go to college. And for what? So a guy
17   could show off to his friends? Was that his way of
18   becoming part of their gang or something? A random act
19   of violence?
20   In the end, I showed that punk. Sure, I sat out of
21   college that next year. Just didn't have the money. I filled
22   my time, painting. Painting with a new rage inside me.
23   Painted pictures so good I sold them on the street. And
24   I made enough money for the first semester of college. I
25   kept painting until the art director at college offered me
26   a full scholarship. That one day, one guy robbed me of a
27   few months of painting, took my chance to win State, but
28   that one day of my life had not stolen my talent ... or my
29   confidence. In the end, I won.

45. Believing in Ghosts
(Guy)

1   MARK: I don't get it. You ask practically anyone if they
2   believe in ghosts and, on some level, most will admit that
3   they do. So why is it that the minute you tell someone
4   that you actually saw one — see one on a daily basis
5   actually — people look at you like you're a psycho? A
6   schizo with talking voices in your head?
7   Well, I am *not* crazy! I swear! See, my brother died
8   about six months ago and ever since then strange things
9   have been happening. I didn't see Patrick at first — just
10   noticed that things weren't where I put them. Clues, I
11   guess, wanting to get my attention. My brother was
12   trying to tell me something, only I was so caught up in
13   convincing myself that I was crazy, I didn't put them all
14   together at first.
15   Then the dreams started. I call them dreams because
16   that's what everyone else calls them. Something that
17   happens in my mind when I'm asleep. Wishful thinking as
18   my mom says. That's when I see Patrick. Only they're
19   not dreams. They're real. He comes to me and talks to
20   me. Tells me things that only he could know. It's not my
21   mind playing tricks on me — it's him! The brother I knew
22   for fifteen years. I close my eyes and he's there waiting.
23   I don't have to fall asleep. I just close my eyes! Why
24   won't anyone believe me?
25   I think Patrick comes to me because he knows I'm not
26   dealing well with his death. I started sneaking drinks to
27   try to cope with it all. He came to me that first night I
28   had a drink. Told me to stop. At first I was so freaked out

1   that I drank more. But he wouldn't go away. He kept
2   coming to me, saying that I had to stop. Finally, I did.
3   See — it's not the alcohol! So why won't anyone
4   believe me? Truth is, people like to say they believe in
5   ghosts ... but when they actually hear of one, they get all
6   freaked out ... I guess I'll keep Patrick to myself ... I
7   don't want to end up in the loony bin!

46. Sisters!
(Girl)

1   MICHELLE: My boyfriend is in love with my sister! I can't
2   believe it took me this long to figure it out. We've been
3   dating almost six months and I finally get it! At first, I
4   thought he was just being nice to her to impress me —
5   you know the kind of guy you can bring home to the
6   family and won't embarrass you or be the cause of you
7   never ever being allowed to date again! I thought he was
8   being the perfect guy!
9   So I wasn't even suspicious when he invited her to
10   watch movies with us or play a game or just plain hang
11   out. Sure, I was annoyed a little, but I kind of thought
12   that maybe he was afraid to be alone with me! It was sort
13   of cute. Or so I thought! What he really wanted was for
14   her to be around. He couldn't have cared less whether I
15   was there or not!
16   It's ridiculous, too, because she wouldn't give him
17   the time of day — normally. But of course because he's
18   mine she actually goes out of her way to be nice to him.
19   She even offers to get him a drink or fix popcorn or junk
20   like that, and my sister doesn't do that for anyone!
21   Usually she expects us to wait on her! Like she's the
22   queen or something. We don't call her Princess Patty for
23   nothing! But is she like that when he's around? *No!* He
24   thinks she's perfect! Not only can I see it in his eyes
25   when I catch him staring at her ... he tells me so!
26   "Your sister is so cool," he says. "I don't know why you
27   don't get along better."
28   I'll tell you why! She's got no heart! If she did, she'd

1 uncross those long, tan legs of hers and get the heck out
2 of my boyfriend's sight! She'd quit playing with him like
3 a cat with a toy! How can I compete with her? Everybody
4 knows that every teenage boy's dream is to be with an
5 "older" woman! She's like caviar and I'm just plain fish
6 guts! Well, if he wants her so much ... he can have her!
7 Believe me, after a week of the true princess, he'd be
8 begging to come back to me!

47. Intuition or Paranoia?
(Girl)

1 KRISTINA: I think something's wrong with me and no one
2 will tell me. Seems like I've had some kind of illness
3 since the day I was born: ear infections, strep throat,
4 constant cough, rash ... I even had mono last year and
5 I've never kissed a guy in my life! Is that fair? I get the
6 kissing disease and I'm like the Virgin Mary!
7 Anyway, I always feel run down and when I look in the
8 mirror I look whiter than the toothpaste that's stuck
9 against the side of the sink. Do my parents know
10 something and they're not telling me? Was I born with
11 some awful disease and they're waiting until I'm old
12 enough to break the news?!
13 I know you probably think I'm being paranoid but I
14 can't help it! I've had a physical every year! Nobody else
15 I know does that! Some of my friends can't even
16 remember the last time they went to the doctor! I'm
17 there like every other week! Is my mom just being ultra-
18 protective or are they checking up on me? Running tests
19 to see how I'm doing and then not telling me!
20 I mean, they can tell a lot from a blood test right? How
21 many kids have their cholesterol checked? Twice a year?
22 Sure, high blood pressure runs in my family and yeah, my
23 mom is a little health food freakish, but doesn't that
24 seem a little suspicious? Who knows what they're really
25 checking me for! Maybe I don't want to know! Maybe it's
26 so bad they know I can't handle it. That's why they've
27 kept me in the dark all these years ...
28 I'm dying ...

1   I know I am ...

2   Oh, for Pete's sake. When are they going to tell me?

3   What are they going to say? Mom and Dad are taking me

4   out Friday night. ... They said it's to celebrate my

5   straight A report card. ... What if that's just a cover

6   up ... What if it's all a lie? I mean, sure, I really got

7   straight A's ... Or did I? It seemed awfully easy. ... Maybe

8   the teachers are in on it. ... What if they just gave me

9   those A's so that Mom and Dad can take me out ...

10   And tell me ... Oh, I really am feeling sick now!

48. Snow Day Blues
(Guy)

1   AUSTIN: This is absolutely insane! We live in a backward
2   podunk town that doesn't have enough sense to buy a
3   snow plow or enough salt for the roads and they expect
4   *us* to go to school thirty minutes longer every day for the
5   rest of the school year? Is it our fault we had fifteen snow
6   days? *No!* Heck, at least half those days we could've gone
7   when they called school off. Why should we, as students,
8   pay for their idiocy?
9   I mean, come on, scrape the roads and get those
10   buses moving. They even canceled one day because we
11   were *supposed* to get snow! There wasn't even a flake in
12   the air when they called off school!
13   So is it fair that I have to suffer through thirty minutes
14   more every day? Is that even legal? Surely there are laws
15   against this! Isn't our day long enough? My brain can't
16   take any more! It'll be fried for sure! I'll get home just in
17   time for dinner ... when am I supposed to get my
18   homework done? I go to work right after dinner. Are they
19   going to pay me for those extra thirty minutes of my life
20   that they're stealing? I didn't sign up for this, no sir! It'll
21   be dark by the time I get home ...
22   What? They're going to add it at the beginning? You've
23   got to be kidding me! They *expect* us to get up even
24   earlier! They're out of their minds! Who are these
25   lunatics? Don't they know a teenager needs sleep ... and
26   plenty of it?!
27   Where's the phone? I'm calling a lawyer!
28

49. Straight-A Student
(Guy)

1   PAUL: I am proud to say that I am a straight-A student! Have
2   been all my life! Not one single B, C, D, or F ... in the
3   subject that really matters to me anyway! Art! I am
4   easily the best artist in the entire school. I can't tell you
5   how many lockers have an original work of mine hanging
6   on the inside of the door!

7   I sketch constantly — on the bus, at home, in class —
8   practically in my sleep. I have hundreds of sketchbooks.
9   Why can't anyone understand that's why I do so badly in
10   everything else? Art is my passion! Not science or math!
11   Who cares about stuff like that? I'm never going to use
12   any of that! The only time I come alive in any of those
13   stupid classes is project time. Everyone else is groaning
14   and complaining and I'm totally excited. Finally a chance
15   to be creative! That's when I get to shine. Every project
16   I've ever done has gotten an A.

17   So I've gotten a few F's on my report card. I'm an
18   artist, not a scholar! Now they're talking about not
19   letting me graduate! Don't they understand that I'm
20   going to be the pride of this school one day? The one that
21   puts them on the map! I've got more talent than anyone
22   here and they're worried about passing me?

23   Why should I be graded on what they think is
24   important? Would they have held back da Vinci or van
25   Gogh? Probably! Well, let them just try to fail me! I'll
26   show them! One day, I'm going to be famous!

27

28

50. Hometown Hero
(Guy)

1   DEREK: I wish the floor would just open up and swallow me.
2   Crack right open and I'd disappear forever. But of course
3   that's not gonna happen. Maybe if I lived in California,
4   right? At least I'd have hopes of an earthquake. But
5   never here. No, I'm stuck. Smile plastered on my face
6   while everyone sings my praises and words like *hero* and
7   *selfless* are floating around my head like dark rain clouds
8   about to drench me.
9   My parents are so proud. Even my little sister is
10   practically beaming, but it could be because she's
11   smiling for the cameraman. I swear the whole town
12   turned out for this stupid event. You'd think I saved a
13   person's life or something ... instead of a dumb dog's.
14   But even that's the real kicker. I didn't even save the
15   dog's life.
16   Everybody thinks because they saw me run out of that
17   abandoned house with the dog in my arms that I'd gone
18   in to rescue the stupid mutt. Yeah, like I'm gonna risk my
19   life for that grungy mongrel. Get real. But no one knows
20   the truth. No one but me and that dumb dog, of course.
21   See, I didn't run in to save the dog — I was already in
22   there. Sneaking a smoke, flicking matches around and
23   watching them burn out. Only the last one must've hit
24   some kind of leftover chemical on the floor or something
25   because there was this huge flash of fire and then the
26   smoke was so thick, I couldn't see to find the door. The
27   whole room was engulfed in flames and I had to crawl
28   around to find my way out.

1   I was coughing like crazy when I finally got to the
2   doorway and that's when I heard it. A low, guttural
3   sound. A growl that sounded like a vicious animal was
4   about to rip me apart.
5   I wasn't going to save that! I thought it was going to
6   attack me! I stood up and started to run toward the back
7   door. The growling noise was right on my heels. I turned
8   to confront it and that's when it happened! The thing
9   charged me, slamming itself into my arms! I still didn't
10   even know it was a dog when I toppled out of the door
11   and we became a tangled mess on the ground.
12   To the few people who were standing outside, it looked
13   like I had leapt from the burning house with the dog in my
14   arms — on purpose! They thought I'd risked my life to
15   save him! What a joke! I thought he was going to kill me!
16   At first I was too dazed to say anything. By the time I
17   could speak, people were hailing me a hero. They even
18   had a television camera shoved in my face. How was I
19   supposed to say anything then?
20   Thing is, I know it's going to come crashing down
21   around me. Sooner or later they're gonna figure out the
22   cause of that fire and they're gonna put two and two
23   together and realize I started it. They can do that, right?
24   The good thing is, they'll never know the truth about
25   that dog. I'll always be the kid that saved that stupid
26   mutt's life. Maybe somehow when the truth comes out
27   about the fire ... they'll have pity on me. I am a hero,
28   after all.

51. Fender Bender
(Girl)

1 HEATHER: I am so totally freaked out. This morning on my
2 way to school, I hit a car! It just popped out of the blue
3 and I hit it! Me in my brand new car! Well, it's not really
4 new, but it's new to me and I absolutely love it! Before
5 today it didn't have a scratch on it! Not one!
6   I just want to cry. I know I should be thankful that at
7 least the other car was OK. No insurance to file. No
8 police report. No damage whatsoever to her stupid little
9 gray truck! But part of me wishes it'd been her truck that
10 got ruined instead of mine!
11   Not that it's ruined. I mean, it's only banged up a little.
12 My friends say it's barely noticeable. Maybe to them! To
13 me, it's like one of those big, red nasty, about-to-burst
14 pimples you get on the end of your nose that everyone
15 can't help starting at!
16   My perfect little car is flawed! I know it was bound to
17 happen sooner or later, but I've only had it three months!
18   Thing's could've been so much worse. I know that.
19 And it is ... just a car ... just a beautiful, baby blue,
20 totally-perfect-for-me car! I can live with a little
21 imperfection, right?
22   I mean, you can't really notice it. Not unless you're
23 looking for it ... not unless ... you're totally *blind!*
24   Oh, who am I kidding? My car is ruined!

52. Cooking Class?
(Guy)

1   JAMIE: You're never gonna believe what's happened to me! I
2   got my schedule today and guess where those idiots in
3   the office put me? Home economics! And they won't
4   switch me out! Do you know what they say about guys
5   who take Home Ec? Well, I'm sure you can imagine and
6   it ain't pretty!

7   It's all my parents fault. They had to go and name me
8   one of those unisex names and so stuff like this happens
9   all the time. First day of class and teachers are like,
10 "Jamie?" "Here," I'll say and they'll look at me funny like
11 I don't know who I am.

12   So now I'm gonna be stuck sewing and cooking and
13 who knows what else! In a room full of girls! I'll probably
14 be the only guy in there!

15   Wait a second! A room full of girls! ... The only guy is
16 me ...

17   You know, now that I think about it, I have always
18 wanted to learn to cook. Heck, there are a *lot* of famous
19 male chefs, right?

20   Who knows where a class like this might lead ...

53. Breaking Up
(Guy)

1   ALEX: This is so whacked! I know girls are like complicated
2   pieces of machinery but I really don't get this! My girlfriend
3   breaks up with me and I'm the bad guy? Every time I see
4   her she's crying and one of her friends is listening to her
5   sob story. Then, they'll see me and I get glared at! What'd
6   I do? She *broke up with me!* Shouldn't I be the one getting
7   all the attention? Getting all the sympathy?
8   What's she doing crying anyway? It's what she wanted.
9   I begged her not to do it. Told her I'd do anything to work
10   things out. But no, she insisted we had to break up. So
11   shouldn't she be happy? She got what she wanted. So
12   why is it that I'm the one smiling and she's the one
13   crying? How mixed up is that?
14   To be honest, I think that's *why* she's so upset. She
15   wanted me to be miserable. Well, I won't give her that
16   satisfaction. I'm not wearing my heart on my sleeve for
17   the whole world to see. I can suffer in private, thank you
18   very much. In fact, I've gone out of my way to be really
19   upbeat in front of everyone. I don't need pity. It's bad
20   enough being the "dumpee."
21   I don't like being the bad guy, though. Maybe I should
22   burst into tears or mope around like her so that everyone
23   will get off my back. How many times do I gotta say this,
24   people? *She broke up with me!*

54. Military School
(Girl)

1　JUSTICE: They're taking my brother away. Pure and simple.
2　　　　　I don't buy that bull for one second that he actually
3　　　　　wants to go to that teenage prison! Nobody chooses to
4　　　　　go to military school! It's for the troublemakers and
5　　　　　potheads — not for guys like my brother!
6　　　　　　My parents are so lame for sending him there! Talk
7　　　　　about overreacting! He gets in trouble once — once in all
8　　　　　these years — and that's it? Last chance! You lose? You're
9　　　　　out the door? Haven't they ever made a mistake? Done
10　　　　something they wished they hadn't? So he messed up. Big
11　　　　deal. Can't they handle it? Do they really get to throw in
12　　　　the whole parenting towel after one minor setback?
13　　　　　They're the ones messing up now. Does that mean I get
14　　　　to ship them off? I don't want Earl to leave. It's bad
15　　　　enough he'll be gone to college in two years, but this is too
16　　　　soon! He promised to teach me to drive. How's he gonna
17　　　　do that from four hours away? They won't even let him
18　　　　come home for the first three months! What if they're
19　　　　treating him bad — beating him or something — how are
20　　　　we even supposed to know? It's a school for bad kids —
21　　　　he won't fit in and they'll pick on him for that! How can
22　　　　anyone in their right mind think that Earl belongs there?
23　　　　　Do they want him learning things from those kinds of
24　　　　kids? What if when he gets out, he's worse than before?
25　　　　What then? Whose fault will that be? Where are they
26　　　　going to ship him off to then?
27　　　　　It's such a crock ... he's my brother ... I don't want him
28　　　　to go ... how are we supposed to be a family without him?

55. Mr. Dee Jay

(Guy)

1   HUNTER: Good morning, Grant High! This is Hunter Holland,
2   your in-the-know school announcer bringing you up-to-
3   date info on the things you *want* to know, *need* to know,
4   and couldn't care less about!
5   First up, all those interested in running needlessly
6   around in a circle getting nowhere are invited to track
7   tryouts immediately after school. Suckers, I mean those
8   that actually make the team, will be posted next Monday.
9   Those poor slobs who don't make the cut are invited to
10 try out for the golf team next Tuesday. Cart fees required
11 at time of enrollment.
12 Next up, teacher tidbits. Mr. Carlson is missing two of
13 his advanced calculus textbooks. He asks that if anyone
14 has one at home doing extra studying that they
15 immediately get psychological help ... I mean, that they
16 return them immediately! No questions asked ... except
17 on those killer tests! Ha, ha!
18 I'm pleased to announce that a theme for prom has
19 finally been determined. And it only took the prom
20 committee four months to do it. Drum roll please. This
21 year's prom theme is called, *"Prom Night 2005."* That's
22 right, folks. Now that's your school dollars at work, isn't
23 it? They must've had help from the creative arts team to
24 come up with that one! Anyhow, be sure to get your
25 tickets now for this lame ... I mean, special night. And
26 don't forget, overpriced photo ops will be available for your
27 enjoyment two hours prior to the start of the actual dance.
28 Today's lunch menu consists of tacos (yes guys, that

1   is actually meat in the bottom of that shell), refried beans
2   that look suspiciously like what my dog, Max, eats, and
3   Mexican rice. The lunchroom staff has once again asked
4   that students *do not* use their pencils as chopsticks on
5   the rice. There are forks available for your convenience.
6   Lastly, all *three* students with a four-point-oh GPA are
7   invited to attend the Beta Club banquet this Friday night.
8   Yes, folks, you can give up a Friday night to hang out with
9   a bunch of ... hey, Miss Wilson ... yeah, I was just about
10   to say that ... a bunch of totally intelligent and totally
11   desirable young people! Oh, and don't forget to bring a
12   side dish.
13   Well, this is Hunter Holland, signing off. Peace out,
14   dudes!

56. Cinderella
(Girl)

1   SANDI: Sometimes I think I'd be better off living on my own.
2   My parents think I'm like their live-in maid or something!
3   I'm a real-life Cinderella, I tell you. Only unlucky for me,
4   there aren't stepsisters to help with the chores. It's me,
5   all me, who has to do everything around here.
6   I even have to get up an hour early every morning
7   before school because there just aren't enough hours in
8   the day to get everything finished. If I let one thing slide
9   it's like an avalanche and I can never seem to get on top
10 again! Not to mention I get grounded every time a chore
11 doesn't get done. I barely have any free time as it is, I
12 sure don't want to spend those precious moments locked
13 in the tower! (OK, my room ... and maybe not *locked*, but
14 *stuck* in it!). I ask you, is there *really* a difference?
15   So I do all the stupid things they tell me — laundry,
16 vacuuming, garbage, empty the dishwasher, dusting. I'm
17 serious. The only thing I don't do is cook or mow! And
18 that's only because, number one: I learned really fast
19 that if I cooked horribly (you know, burned stuff or left
20 important ingredients out) I didn't have to do it, and
21 number two: My mom saw a TV special on some kid who
22 lost his leg in a mower accident (so Dad is stuck with
23 that one!). You might think that proves my parents at
24 least care about me, but I think that just proves that
25 they don't want their maid laid up with a bum or missing
26 leg, unable to keep the house up!
27   I should mention that at least they pay me a fairly
28 generous allowance. Which would be pretty sweet if I ever

1   had a minute to spend any of it *or* if they didn't make me
2   put ninety percent of it back into my bank account! I
3   think I'll have college paid for before I even graduate from
4   high school!
5   I swear living on my own would be ten times better. I do
6   it all anyway. And I wouldn't have to pick up after them!

57. Kissing in the Hall
(Girl)

1   MARYANNE: I don't understand what the big deal is. So I got
2   caught kissing a guy in the hall. I swear teachers in this
3   school overreact about everything. It's like they've
4   completely forgotten what it's like to be young and in
5   love. How are we supposed to make it all day long
6   without so much as a little peck? Who's it hurting as long
7   as I get to class on time?

8   What a bunch of prudes we've got around here. Now
9   I'm facing a Saturday detention just because of one little
10   act of affection? I guess they want us to be as cold and
11   heartless as they are! I doubt my science teacher has
12   kissed a guy in her life. Who'd want to kiss a soured up
13   face like that?

14   What am I supposed to do? Avoid my boyfriend like the
15   plague? Seeing him in between classes is the only thing
16   that gets me through the day!

17   I can't believe that Mr. Crabapple turned me in.
18   Doesn't he have something better to do than patrol the
19   halls? Shouldn't he be grading papers or something other
20   than ruining students' lives?

21   Now I'm gonna be in big trouble and it's all his fault.
22   My mom's gonna flip when she hears I got detention.
23   She'll probably ground me from seeing Corey for a
24   month — her standard punishment for anything I do
25   wrong! Then when are we supposed to kiss? In our
26   dreams?! I swear the whole world is against us! I guess I
27   might as well hang it up now and become a nun!

58. A Painful Memory
(Girl)

1   JANICE: It was one of those nights I'll remember for the rest
2   of my life. I woke up ready to cry because of this stabbing
3   pain radiating through my head. It only took a second for
4   me to figure out why: earache. I've had enough in my
5   lifetime to know right away it was a whopper, too. Holding
6   the side of my head, trying not to cry out, I made my way
7   out of my room, looking for my mom. I knew she'd put the
8   drops in my ear that would numb the pain.
9   I went to her room. Empty. Both she and Dad were
10   gone, which was strange since the clock beside their bed
11   read three o'clock a.m. Where would they be at this
12   hour? They'd been home when I went to bed. Surely they
13   didn't leave without telling any of us.
14   I headed toward the living room and that's when I heard
15   them. Out on the porch. Their voices were muffled. I
16   couldn't tell what they were saying but I knew it was them.
17   I moved closer. I wasn't eavesdropping. Really. I was going
18   to go out there. To tell them about my ear hurting.
19   My hand was on the doorknob ready to turn it when I
20   froze. Mom was crying. Sobbing, really. "Please don't
21   leave us. Please don't leave us," she said.
22   Tears sprang to my eyes and I stood there shaking.
23   Not knowing what to do. Why was Mom so upset? My
24   dad went on business trips all the time. What was the big
25   deal now? My hand dropped to my side.
26   I don't know how long I stood there, listening to my
27   mother crying, pain shooting through my head and my
28   heart. I wanted to go to her but somehow I knew I

1   shouldn't. I was too young to understand the full impact
2   of what I'd heard. But old enough to understand it was
3   private ... and very important.
4   And it was. Important enough to change my life forever.
5   My dad left the next day. Not on a business trip like I'd
6   thought. But left for good. I haven't seen him since.

59. One Hundred Years Old
(Girl)

1   BETTY: I'm gonna look like a hundred-year-old grandma! I
2   swear! I wish I'd never complained about not being able
3   to hear the teacher, 'cause now this idiot doctor is saying
4   I need a hearing aid! Is he crazy? Where'd he get his
5   medical license? The Internet? Can't he see how *young* I
6   am? Nobody my age wears a stupid hearing aid! What
7   are they trying to do to me? Keep me from having a
8   boyfriend the rest of my life? Who's gonna date a girl that
9   looks like their grandma? They might as well put a sign
10   around my neck that says *old maid* now!
11   I can't go to school with a big old peachy looking thing
12   sticking out of my ear! I'd rather not hear than have to
13   wear one of those awful things! I can just read the
14   textbook more. I mean really, how much does anyone
15   listen to the teacher anyway?
16   Of course, it would be nice to not have to ask my
17   friends to repeat things all the time. They get really mad
18   sometimes when I keep saying, "Huh?" I can't tell you
19   how often I just nod and smile and have no idea what I'm
20   agreeing to. Usually I just keep turning my head so my
21   one good ear can pick up the conversation. I guess it'd
22   be nice to not have to do that anymore.
23   And they do have these new contraptions out that are
24   much smaller than the one my grandma has. My mom
25   swears that with my hair down, you'll hardly be able to
26   see it. And the doctor promises that they don't squeak
27   like they used to. This one would be high tech. Digital
28   and all. They even have this mute function where I can

1   tune everyone out! Now that'd be great when my little
2   brother, William, is bugging me!
3   You know, now that I think about it ... maybe having a
4   hearing aid won't be so bad after all!

60. Split Personality
(Guy)

1   TREY: I live a split life. On one hand I'm this tough guy that
2   everyone in school fears. And I mean everyone. I get away
3   with murder because they're too afraid to say anything. I
4   work hard at keeping up that side of me. You know,
5   getting in fights every now and then, just to make sure no
6   one ever sees me as weak. I like it that way, that's why I
7   never let anyone see the other side of who I am.

8   I drive twenty minutes to the next county just so no
9   one will ever find out what I do in my free time. See, I'm
10   a volunteer at the animal shelter. Three times a week
11   after school. I get to walk the dogs, play with the kittens
12   and occasionally bring them home until they're adopted.
13   It's a hard job sometimes because we get some animals
14   in pretty bad shape. Some of them don't make it. My
15   friends would die if they saw how tore up I get over an
16   animal I may only have seen for a day or so.

17   People are cruel. You wouldn't believe how horrible
18   they treat animals. I just don't get it. How can you hurt
19   something that is so small and defenseless? What pigs!

20   Anyway, you can see why I could never let anyone
21   know this about me. I'd be the one on the other side of
22   the punch for sure! And that would never work. I have a
23   reputation to uphold, after all.

61. Vegetables?
(Guy)

1   BLAKE: My mother is trying to turn me into a rabbit! She's
2   on the no meat kick and thinks that our whole family
3   should become leaf eaters! Problem is, I can't stand
4   vegetables. If God wanted me to be a rabbit he'd have
5   given me long ears and a cute little furry face. How am I
6   supposed to survive on total green? Broccoli, lettuce,
7   *asparagus!* Nobody eats that stuff!
8   Oh, she throws in some color every now and then.
9   Orange carrots. Yellow corn. And all the fruit I can eat ...
10   oh boy! My mother is a fruit, I tell you. I want a big, juicy
11   steak — you know, food that takes more than one chew
12   to go down. Something I can sink my teeth into.
13   My dad agrees to all this just to humor her. We know
14   Mom goes through these kinds of phases all the time. It
15   wasn't too long ago that we ate Chinese food — on pillows
16   on the floor, mind you. Then there was the time that she
17   was anti-electric! Wanted us to use candles and hand
18   wash everything. Oh, and the time she thought the
19   microwave was killing us with these silent cancer waves! I
20   didn't get to make popcorn for a month! And do you know
21   how long it takes to actually heat something up in the
22   oven? Of course not! Every other normal person zaps it in
23   the microwave! She gets all these strange ideas from TV.
24   Every time the news has a special report, our lives change!
25   So I guess it's fair to assume that this too will pass.
26   Some other weird phase will enter my mother's life. Like
27   giving up cars or something. I can just see me walking
28   the two miles to school everyday!

1	My mother always keeps us guessing. It's not totally a
2	bad thing, though. It certainly makes life interesting. I
3	guess you could say she's overzealous. Way too excited
4	about stuff. But all of her life changes make me want to
5	go through a phase of my own. It's called "No Television
6	Specials for Mom." Maybe then things would be normal
7	around here.

62. Ready, Set … Leave!
(Guy)

1 KURT: Well, here I am getting ready to audition for the part
2   that could one day make me famous! Everything has to
3   start somewhere, right? And who knows where this
4   commercial could lead me? Sure, it's just a local news
5   thing, but it could be my chance of getting discovered!
6   I'm a shoe-in, too. Just look at the competition. Does
7   little curly redhead think that anyone would buy that
8   innocent, freckled-face look? Besides, the part will clearly
9   be better if a guy plays it. More believable.
10   And what about that dude over there with the hair
11   down to his shoulders? I hardly think he represents the
12   all-American boy. At least let's hope not. He's been to
13   the bathroom three times already. Probably popping
14   some kind of pill or something. Do we really need a
15   druggie for this part?
16   Of course, Mr. Jock just had to wear his letter jacket,
17   didn't he? He probably sleeps in the stupid thing. Good
18   thing is, he's probably too dumb to read his lines all the
19   way through. I can see him still trying to memorize them.
20   Does Mr. Jockey-Wocky need help with the big words? He
21   definitely shouldn't be any problem. Besides he'll
22   probably have to leave in time for football practice.
23   Speaking of which … what *is* taking so long? We've
24   been sitting out here for almost an hour. They've only
25   taken one person back. Don't they know we have better
26   things to do than sit around here all day? Especially
27   these other poor souls who will waste their time only to
28   be told to go home anyway. I kind of feel sorry for them.

1   They don't even have a clue it's coming. Look at their
2   faces: excitement, anticipation, fear. All mixed together.
3   You can tell they've never done this before. Never
4   auditioned. Never performed. I'm glad it's not *my* first
5   time. I'm practically an old hat at this. I did audition for
6   two other parts, after all.
7   And I would've gotten them, too, only I think at the last
8   minute they changed their mind and went a whole other
9   way. You know how things like that happen. Showbiz. It's
10   a crazy world. You just have to get used to it.
11   Oh look! Here comes someone now. She's holding a
12   clipboard. She's looking us over. This is it! I can tell
13   she's going to pick me next. I clear my throat, so I can
14   get my voice box ready ... I race through the lines in my
15   head ... yup, I know them all ...
16   Wait a second ... she's turning back around ... leaving.
17   ... Did she even say anything? I got so lost going over my
18   lines in my head, I didn't hear her. ... I just knew she was
19   going to call me. ... Everyone's getting up. ... They're
20   leaving. ... Where are they going?
21   *"Wait!* I haven't even auditioned!" I say out loud
22   without even realizing it.
23   "Dude," Mr. Football says. "They picked someone
24   else. Better luck next time."
25   *"Better luck next time?* Are you crazy? I can't go
26   through this again! It's agony, pure agony! Being treated
27   like a number ... a piece of meat ... Hey, is that an ad for
28   another audition?"
29   I grab the paper out of Mr. Football's hands. "Come on,
30   if we hurry, we'll make it just in time for final call!"

63. Motorcycle Mania
(Guy)

1 ROSS: My mother is being completely paranoid. She thinks
2   that just because I don't want to drive a tank that I'm
3   going to end up splattered all over the road somewhere!
4   It's so unfair! I've been driving safely — no accidents, no
5   speeding tickets, not even a parking ticket — for a year!
6   What do I have to do to prove to her that I'm a good driver?
7   A good driver who deserves to drive what *he* wants!

8   And I want a motorcycle! I've got it all picked out and
9   I've saved all of the money to buy it. So why can't I
10   have it? Lots of people ride motorcycles and they don't
11   end up as a clump on a semitruck's wheels! (Mom's
12   words, not mine!)

13   I'm seventeen! I should be able to do what I want. And
14   I would, too, if she just wouldn't drop me from the
15   insurance for doing it! It's like this power she's got over
16   me. She knows I could never afford to pay for insurance
17   without being on her policy! How can she use that
18   against me? Isn't that like blackmail or something?

19   I just can't live without one! How can I get her to see
20   how totally awesome riding a motorcycle is? The wind
21   blowing against you ... the freedom ... the speed ... *not*
22   that I'd speed! I wouldn't! I'd obey all the traffic rules *and*
23   I'd wear a helmet. *Every* time. Even in the neighborhood
24   and just to go to the store ... even when it's like a
25   hundred out and the helmet makes you sweat like a
26   pig ... I'd wear it! I would!

27   Come on, Mom! I could have an accident in a car! I
28   could! ... *No,* I'm not saying I will ... of course I drive

1   careful, Mom. I swear. I've never had a speeding ticket,

2   remember! Yeah, I know that could mean I just haven't

3   been caught ... but I haven't been ... *No,* I haven't been

4   *speeding!* Why are you twisting everything I say? *I just*

5   *want a motorcycle!*

6   ... Wait! I didn't mean to yell ... oh, come on! You can't

7   ground me for that! *What?* I can't drive for a month? How

8   can I live without driving?!

64. Graduation Blues
(Girl)

1   TRISTA: This party is going to be completely and totally
2   lame. I doubt anyone will even stay at it once they realize
3   that my parents intend to be permanent fixtures! Who's
4   gonna want to stay at a *kindergarten* graduation party!
5   They might as well have put up a stupid pin-the-tail-on-
6   the-donkey poster and had us bob for apples!
7   Nobody graduates high school and goes to a
8   *chaperoned* party! Why are my parents being so stubborn
9   about this? I knew I should've just said, "No, thank you"
10   when they offered to throw this thing. Of course, I'd
11   hoped that at some point they would come to their
12   senses and realize that *no one* has their parents at their
13   graduation party! What are they trying to do? Get me
14   laughed at for the rest of my life?
15   I guess I can be thankful that I'll be in college in just
16   a few short months and that I'm going almost four hours
17   away. No one will know me there. No one will know what
18   a lame-o I am! They won't know I hosted the worst
19   graduation party ever!
20   Maybe I should just get sick. Start barfing on the way
21   back from the ceremonies. Who'd be disappointed? Not
22   me! I could just hang out here ... alone ... alone on my
23   graduation day! Oh, that's lamer than the party! Maybe I
24   can just get my parents to hide out all night in their room!

65. Coolest Job in Town
(Guy)

1 GRADY: I've got the coolest job in town! It's so unfair that
2   they won't let me work more hours! Stupid labor laws!
3   Don't they realize that I should be paying *them* for
4   working? It's so awesome! See, I work at the movie
5   theater and I get all the popcorn and soda I want for free!
6   Which is great, but the totally awesome part is that I can
7   watch *all* the movies before anyone else. It's like I'm a VIP!
8   Sneak preview nights are on Thursday. All the
9   employees can stay after work and watch the newest
10   releases! Now how cool is that? Plus, I can go to any
11   movie I want — *for free!* Now to most people that might
12   not be that big a deal, but I'm like the biggest movie fan
13   ever! I own two hundred fifty-five videos and one hundred
14   DVDs! *I love movies!*
15   I've probably watched some of my favorites about
16   twenty-five times each! So of course working for the
17   theater is like a dream come true! I've seen every single
18   movie that's come out in the last six months. Every one!
19   People always switch to my line so they can ask my
20   opinion because I'm like the town movie guru!
21   Just think how much money I'd be paying to do all this
22   movie watching! This job is saving me a bundle! Oh, I forgot
23   the best part. I also get a free ticket for a friend. So *voila!*
24   Free dates right here! No more shelling out twenty bucks for
25   a movie date! I'm off scot-free and my date doesn't have a
26   clue! Thinks I'm a big spender taking her to dinner *and* a
27   movie! How many other poor slobs can do that?
28   I swear I might just keep this job forever!

66. Junior Miss Pageant
(Girl)

1 ALLISON: What am I doing here? I can't sing, can't dance,
2 don't play the piano. I don't fit in with these beautiful
3 girls. More than half of them are cheerleaders! Why did I
4 ever let my friend talk me into joining the Junior Miss
5 Pageant? Did I need total humiliation in my life?
6   Look at them! Perfect teeth, perfect hair, perfect
7 makeup! And *they* did their own! I had to have the lady
8 at the mall do mine. I've never even seen so many
9 brushes and tubes of stuff in my life! Do they really go
10 through that every day? I guess beauty does have a price.
11   To be honest, though, these chicks would be beautiful
12 without all that junk. Their faces are picture perfect.
13 High cheekbones. Flawless skin. If I looked like that
14 naturally I sure wouldn't hide it behind all that goop. Me,
15 I need the goop. I can see that now. 'Cause this girl
16 staring back at me in the mirror — *wow!* She's totally zit
17 and freckle-free! My skin is this beautiful even color —
18 not splotchy at all. And my eyes! I've never noticed how
19 blue they are. From a distance, I may actually look like I
20 belong up here with these other girls!
21   Of course, I still can't dance or sing or be graceful like
22 them. That's why I picked this stupid clown routine for
23 talent. An intentional goofball is better than an
24 unintentional one, right?! That way, if I trip or walk funny,
25 they'll think it's all part of the act!
26   I just have to make it through the next few minutes.
27 Stand up here smiling while the judges mark their final
28 choices. I guess it hasn't been so bad after all. The girls

1   have been really nice. And for a few minutes, when I was

2   out there in my gown swirling around for everyone to see,

3   I kind of felt like a princess. I guess that's how these girls

4   feel all the time — for me, it was like the moment of a

5   lifetime! I may never be a Junior Miss, but I won't forget

6   this feeling for a long, long time!

67. Princess Grace
(Girl)

1   HOPE: Everyone is talking about me. And when I say
2   everyone, I mean it. At least everyone here at this school.
3   They are whispering my name and giggling while under
4   their breaths they are thanking God that they are not me!
5   "Miss Grace," they call me or just "Grace" if they're in a
6   hurry. It's been this way for almost a week. I keep waiting
7   for someone else around here to do something utterly
8   humiliating so that the school will forget about me, but
9   of course it's been an uneventful week. Not one thing to
10   take the pressure off me. Any other week, we would've
11   had at least three major events by now ... but no, fate
12   just won't let me off the hook that easily!
13   I just wish I could turn back time one week! That's all
14   I ask! Seven measly little days. Then I'd know better than
15   to go to that stupid assembly we had at school. I
16   would've faked being sick and stayed home. Even though
17   Mrs. Johnson said that our grades would suffer if we
18   missed the performance. A bad grade ... so what? I can
19   live through that!
20   By now you're probably wondering what the heck
21   happened that horrible day. I can't believe I'm even going
22   to tell you — relive it one more time! I swear everyone
23   must have a video replay in their heads because every
24   day I hear another embarrassing detail!
25   Anyway, there I was, singing my little heart out with the
26   chorus — the advanced chorus, I might add — when it
27   came time for my solo. I started climbing as
28   inconspicuously as I could down from the top riser. That's

1 when it happened. My heel got caught on the edge of the
2 second step and I toppled, head over heels all the way
3 down to the bottom. Of course it scared me! The wind
4 sure was knocked out of me, so I just lay on the floor
5 trying to figure out if I'd broken anything. Maybe if I had
6 broken something (like my neck!), everyone would feel
7 guilty about calling me names, but of course I wasn't lucky
8 enough to be taken out on a stretcher! Oh no! I just lay
9 there, dazed and confused, while the whole school stared
10 at my underwear! That's right! My skirt was up around my
11 neck! Exposing all for the school to see!

12   The teacher ran over and tried to cover me up, but it was
13 too late. Everyone had seen my tiger-striped panties! And
14 the fact that I'd cheated and wore knee-high stockings that
15 day! I looked like someone's warped grandma!

16   So you can see it's going to take a pretty big scandal
17 to top that! I just keep praying that soon some other
18 poor soul will do something totally embarrassing. I guess
19 some might think that makes me a bad person, wishing
20 ill on someone else, but I'm just ready to pass the
21 "Princess Grace" title on to someone else!

68. Pet Frog

(Girl)

1　TIFFANY: I've never thought of myself as an animal rights
2　　　　activist. Seriously. I'm a meat eater, for Pete's sake. So I'm
3　　　　sure it's hard for the teacher to understand why I'm acting
4　　　　this way. It's hard for me to understand. All I know is that
5　　　　when I looked into Freddie's little beady eyes, I knew there
6　　　　was no way I could cut him up.
7　　　　　It's completely insane, too, because it doesn't take a rocket
8　　　　scientist to know that Freddie's already been dead for a long,
9　　　　long time. Preserved until just this moment by that smelly
10　　　murky liquid he's been floating around in. But it just doesn't
11　　　feel right to slice up his little green body. It's disrespectful.
12　　　　I can just picture him hopping around the pond, making
13　　　those cute little froggie noises. What'd they do, snatch him
14　　　up in the middle of the night? Did they kill him right away or
15　　　feed him flies until he got big and fat and then send a little
16　　　froggie hit man?
17　　　　How can I cut open his body, dig around in his insides all
18　　　in the name of science? I don't plan on being a scientist or
19　　　a vet, why do I care what froggie parts look like? How am I
20　　　ever going to use that in my life? So why should I treat
21　　　Freddie's body like a piece of meat? He's staring at me! I
22　　　can't cut him up!
23　　　　So now I have to take an F on this lab. Can she do that?
24　　　Don't I have some kind of right to refuse to be a mutilator!
25　　　What kind of sick kids do they want us to be? Shouldn't it
26　　　bother them that Greg over there is practically drooling at
27　　　being able to slice up an animal that way? That's way more
28　　　disturbing than me refusing to do it!
29　　　　So I'll take that F thank you very much! An F for Freddie!

69. Softhearted Sucker
(Girl)

1   SHERI: I am *so* gullible! My mother has always said it but I
2   never really believed her until now. I truly got taken
3   advantage of and I have the empty wallet to prove it. I could
4   live with that, since it was my decision to hand over the
5   money, but I was dumb enough to take some things from
6   home, too! What was I thinking? I knew this big stupid
7   heart of mine was going to get me in trouble one day!

8   It all started Monday when Morgan came to school with
9   a huge bruise on her arm. She was crying in the bathroom
10   and when I asked her what happened she told me that her
11   father hits her. All the time. I couldn't believe it! I wanted
12   to run and get a teacher, tell someone who could help her,
13   but she wouldn't let me. She said she was terrified that
14   her father would kill her if he found out she'd told anyone.
15   That's when she told me her plan to run away. In my
16   defense, I tried to talk her out of it. Tried to get her to tell
17   someone instead. But she was so afraid.

18   So I bought into her idea. She could run away to safety.
19   At least she wouldn't get hit anymore, right? She said she
20   knew someone in Florida who would take her in *if* she
21   could just get there. She talked of hitchhiking. I couldn't
22   let her do that! I've heard horror stories of sick men who
23   pick up teenage girls! So what choice did I have?

24   I told her to meet me later that night and I'd help her
25   out. Right after school I went to the bank and took all of
26   my money out of savings. Two hundred dollars. Not a lot
27   to some, but a whole lot to me! And I rushed around the
28   house stuffing things I thought she'd need into a bag.

1   Snacks, magazines, toiletries ... everything I could think
2   of! Basically, I stole things out of my house to give to
3   Morgan. I know I could've asked my mom and she
4   would've given those things to me, but I couldn't! Then
5   she'd ask questions and I'd promised not to tell a soul!
6   All in all it's not a bad story. Had Morgan truly needed
7   the help, I would be feeling pretty good right about now.
8   Proud of my whole Good Samaritan act. Problem is, on
9   Monday morning I ran into Morgan's sister, Patricia, who
10   told me that Morgan really did run away this weekend!
11   Not to get away from an abusive father but to run off with
12   her twenty-year-old boyfriend! And get this! They used
13   the money I gave them to get married! *Get married!*
14   Oh, and you know that bruise she was all upset about?
15   Patricia says she got it from the wonderful man I helped
16   her marry! I swear, I'm never helping another person out
17   for as long as I live! This softhearted sucker is closed for
18   business!

70. Exchange Student
(Girl)

1   JERRIE: *Hola! Uno, dos, tres* ... Oh, this is never going to
2   work! I can't just count to the poor girl! What made Mom
3   and Dad think that we needed an exchange student
4   anyway? For a whole year! I can't speak Spanish, and
5   who knows how well she can speak English? They say
6   they have to be able to communicate well, but I met a
7   guy last year in school who could barely understand
8   a word we said! What if she's like that? How can I share
9   a room with a person I can't even talk to?
10   At first I was really excited. I figured it was the closest
11   thing to a sister I was ever going to get. I pictured us as
12   big pals. Instant best friends. Staying up all night.
13   Talking about boys. Sister stuff.
14   Mom and Dad showed me her picture and she looks
15   nice enough. But what if she's not? What if she's mean
16   and starts yelling at me in words I can't understand?
17   She's going to be here in just one week. *One week!*
18   I've been trying to learn a little Spanish just in case, but
19   it sure is hard. Nothing makes sense in that language!
20   What am I supposed to do? Walk around all day with a
21   Spanish-English dictionary? I can just imagine how long
22   it's going to take to say a sentence by the time I look up
23   every single word!
24   What if she steals my boyfriend? I know how guys are
25   about a pretty face and an accent. We had a girl move
26   from up north last year and the guys just ogled her to
27   death. They couldn't get enough of her northern kind of
28   speaking. This will be ten times worse! Any foreign

1   language sounds sexy!

2   And what if my friends like her better than me? I'll
3   introduce her around and then she'll be the one getting
4   invited to parties and I'll be left behind. Everybody will
5   want to be around her, hear about the way things are in
6   her country. Basically she'll be the new meat and I'll be
7   the reduced, gotta-eat-by-such-and-such-a-date kind!

8   How am I gonna talk my parents out of this? How can
9   I convince them that this is all a big mistake? How can
10   I ... oh, look. A letter. For me. It's from her. She's so
11   excited about coming ...she sounds so nice ... I know I'm
12   going to love her! Oh, I just can't wait for her to come!
13   We're going to be like sisters!

71. Sardines
(Guy)

1   CHANDLER: I don't think I can unbend my knees. Seriously.
2   About five hundred miles back I think I lost the ability to
3   straighten up. I've been scrunched in the backseat of this
4   stinking Volkswagen Rabbit for three days now, and if I don't
5   get some serious stretching time soon I'm going to be bent
6   like a pretzel for life. Then the stupid money that my parents
7   saved by driving this *gas efficient* piece of junk will all be for
8   nothing! They'll be handing over a lot more than that in
9   doctor's bills to get their crippled son straightened out!

10   I can just see me now in one of those slingy bed
11   contraptions where they'll attach things to my legs to try to
12   pull them straight! I assume my brother and sister will be
13   stretched out beside me since they're scrunched back here
14   with me, too! Yes, folks, in case you thought you didn't hear
15   that right, there are *three* of us normal-sized (except for me,
16   who is actually taller than most guys my age) teenagers in
17   the backseat of this mini-sized car! We look like a stinking
18   clown car every time we stop (which is *not* very often, I might
19   add) and get out to eat or get gas. No one expects to see
20   three people climb out from back here! Most intelligent
21   people would hardly expect one!

22   And it's starting to smell back here, too. Sweat and feet.
23   Yuck. And Jim keeps trying to sleep on me, and when he
24   does, he drools! Talk about nasty! This is absolutely the trip
25   from you know where! It certainly is the *"memorable"* trip my
26   mom promised! Nothing could get this out of my head,
27   that's for sure!

28   Next time my family goes on a "budget" family vacation,
29   they can count me out!

72. She-Devil
(Girl)

1   HALEY: My sister is the spawn of the devil! I'm serious. She's
2   completely evil. She goes out of her way to be mean to me
3   and I'm four years older than her! You'd think she'd be
4   afraid of me, but *no!* She knows that if I touch her *I'll* get
5   in trouble, not her. So she pushes me and pushes me until
6   I'm ready to snap! She's driving me crazy!
7   You think I'm kidding but I'm not. She's like an angel
8   to everyone else. Cute little blonde-haired, blue-eyed girl
9   who smiles sweetly and is super polite: "Yes, ma'am. No
10   ma'am." — *Gag me!* The second no one else is around
11   the horns come out and her eyes turn red. She steals my
12   stuff — then breaks it! Eavesdrops on my conversations
13   and then blabs my intimate stuff all over the
14   neighborhood! She makes messes that I have to clean
15   up! And she always forgets to do her *one* chore — empty
16   the dishwasher — until it's time for her to get in bed and
17   then Mom'll say it's too late for her to stay up and do it
18   and I get stuck doing it! How fair is that?
19   I thought maybe now that I have my driver's license
20   she'd be nice to me. You know, so I'd take her places.
21   *Wrong!* She's meaner than ever! She knows that I'd do
22   just about anything to not get grounded from driving, so
23   it's like she can get away with murder!
24   Who would've ever thought I'd be slave to a twelve-
25   year-old brat? She rules my life. I thought that was *my*
26   right! I am the oldest child, after all. Don't I have a divine
27   right to boss *her* around?
28   Well, not around here apparently! I can't wait to move

1   out. Then we'll see who the she-devil picks on! Maybe
2   then my parents will see what she's really like! They'll
3   finally see who the *real* angel is! *Me!*

73. You Can't Turn My Room into a Study!

(Guy)

1 STUART: I don't think I'm being unreasonable. I don't.
2 This has been my room for seventeen years — how can
3 they just expect me to pack it up and put my stuff
4 in storage? Geesh, I'm just going off to college, don't
5 they ever expect me to come back? I don't want to
6 sleep in the guest room! I'm not a guest! This is my
7 home ... my room. They've already pulled down my
8 wallpaper. Couldn't even wait for me to have my foot in
9 the door at college. It's like they've been waiting all
10 their lives for this!

11   I guess I thought things would stay the same.
12 Whenever I'd visit I'd still have all my stuff here. Right
13 where I left it. Not in some smelly old box in the attic! My
14 stuff doesn't belong up there!

15   I mean, look at this hole in the wall. I remember when I
16 made that. Sixth grade. I didn't get picked for the
17 basketball team and I was really upset. I threw open my
18 door and it stuck in the wall. It's been that way all these
19 years and *now* they want to fix it? *Repaint* the whole room?
20 Put up some kind of tacky wallpaper? I don't think so!

21   And what about this spot on the carpet? This is where
22 I spilled paint when I was painting my science fair
23 project. How can they rip out the carpet and put in
24 hardwood floors? *I got an A on that project!* Does that
25 mean nothing to them?

26   My room can't be a study. It's a bedroom. *My*
27 bedroom. You don't have a closet in a study, do you? *Do*

1	*you?* What the heck is a *study* anyway? We've never had
2	one before, so why do we need one now?
3	I know. There's just one thing to do. It's brilliant
4	really. I should've thought of it earlier ... I won't go to
5	college. I won't. I'll just stay here. Get a job. Keep my
6	room. Keep things the same. Look. I'm unpacking right
7	now. Putting my stuff back. Just the way I like it. See?
8	It looks better now, doesn't it? *Doesn't it?*
9	I mean, they can't force me to leave, right?
10	I'm their kid.
11	They have to keep me, right?

74. Holiday Blues
(Girl)

1   GLORIA: I think I should be able to decide who I want to
2   spend Thanksgiving with. It's a stupid holiday where
3   people stuff themselves with food. Why does it matter if
4   I spend it with my friend instead of my family? My
5   parents are being completely unreasonable. This is the
6   chance of a lifetime! A trip to Florida with my best friend
7   for a whole week. I can't believe they're not going to let
8   me go!
9   It's not like I'm anti-family or anything, but come on,
10   it's Turkey Day for crying out loud! It's a hyped-up day for
11   pigging out! Why do I *have* to be a part of it? Sure, my
12   aunts and uncles and all of their whiny little kids will be
13   here ... so what? That's just one more reason why I
14   shouldn't be. I get stuck at the "kids'" table and end up
15   having to entertain the snot-nosed brats. Of course, my
16   parents have a blast. They're at the "adult" table where
17   all the fun is! I'm stuck watching my cousins shove peas
18   up each other's noses!
19   How can they take this from me? My one chance at a
20   *great* Thanksgiving! One I'd never forget. Louise says the
21   hotel has *three* pools *and* it's *on the beach!* The worst
22   part is, if I don't get to go she's going to ask Penny!
23   *Penny!* They'll come back best friends, and where will
24   that leave me? Friendless, thank you very much, and it
25   will be all my parents' fault!
26   I've just got to go. I do. I can picture me and Louise
27   on the beach. Checking out guys. Playing a little sand
28   volleyball. Getting a tan to show off when school starts

1   back up. Everyone will be so jealous. It's the vacation of

2   a lifetime. ... Sure, I've been to the beach before, but

3   never for Thanksgiving and never with my *best friend!* It

4   would be *so much fun!*

5   I don't care that Grandma's flying in from Washington.

6   I'll send her a postcard. She's always mixing me up with

7   one of my cousins anyway. She won't even miss me.

8   Besides she'll be back for a week in the summer. I can

9   see her then.

10   Isn't it about time I got to do what I want? Haven't I

11   suffered through enough family get-togethers? Haven't

12   I ...

13   What?

14   I'm getting bumped up to the "adult" table? For

15   real? Me?

16   Oh, this is going to be the best Thanksgiving ever!

75. Sleeping on the Job
(Girl)

1   GINA: I just don't get it, God. I've always done everything
2   you want. I don't lie, cheat, steal, do drugs, drink. I don't
3   even talk back to my parents, and for a kid like me that's
4   practically a miracle! And you should know, right?
5   I have friends who are a hundred times worse than I
6   would ever be. They don't even go to church, God. But
7   we do. *We do!* We haven't missed a Sunday for practically
8   my whole life. So why did this have to happen to us? To
9   our family?
10   Landon was only eight years old, God. *Eight years old.*
11   He was too young to suffer like that. Too young to die.
12   How could you take him from us?
13   We're falling apart now. It's like all the life has been
14   sucked out of our family. There's no laughter. No
15   emotion. Nobody wants to feel anything any more.
16   What are you doing up there? Sleeping on the job?
17   Watching cable? What? Why didn't you hear me when I
18   prayed about this? Why didn't you heal him? It wasn't
19   much to ask ... there are plenty of old people you can
20   take, aren't there? Why did it have to be him? He never
21   hurt anyone. Never caused any trouble.
22   I mean sure, he was a pain sometimes. But what little
23   brother isn't? I never wanted him to die, God. Never! Not
24   even when he and his friends made copies of my diary
25   and spread them all over school! Or when he wrapped his
26   bloody arm in my favorite shirt. I knew he didn't mean it.
27   Landon was never mean on purpose. Just mischievous.
28   And he really had this heart for bugs. He would spend

1   all night collecting a whole jar full and then just let them
2   go. He didn't want them to die stuck in a jar, God. Most
3   kids don't even think of things like that. See, Landon was
4   different.
5   I still can't believe he's gone. Sometimes I just sit on
6   his bed and think about him. It scares me when I can't
7   picture him exactly the way he used to be. I'm afraid I'm
8   going to forget him. Forget how he looked. I just miss
9   him so much.
10   He's probably up in heaven chasing after butterflies ...
11   you do have butterflies, don't you? Because Landon will
12   be miserable if you don't. Miserable like us. I wouldn't
13   want that for him. I know he's happy now. Out of pain.
14   It's better for him, right? Maybe one day we'll be able to
15   think about him without being sad.
16   Look. It's his bug jar. And his net. Maybe I'll catch a
17   few ... just for fun ... and then let them go ... for Landon. ...
18   I miss you, little brother.

76. There Goes the Streak!
(Girl)

1   JENNA: Have you ever done something risky? Something so
2   wild and stupid that you immediately regretted it? Of
3   course you have! Haven't we all done at least one thing
4   that we wish we could erase from our past? One thing
5   that we worry will come back to haunt us when we least
6   expect it? Well, if you don't worry about things like that,
7   I sure do!
8   See, in one daring moment, I put myself out there for
9   total embarrassment! I will never forget that moment for
10   the rest of my life! There I was, buck-naked, streaking
11   through my best friend's basement — on a dare, of
12   course! It's not like I just strip and streak for no
13   reason! — when her mother opens the basement door
14   and sees me — in *all my glory* — zipping past her!
15   I don't know who was more shocked! Me or her! It's
16   funny how fast that free feeling I had dropped to the pit
17   of my stomach like a boulder. Everyone started dying
18   laughing! Not that they weren't laughing before (what do
19   you think made her mother come down in the first
20   place?), but this was real hee-hawing! I just wanted to
21   melt into that cold concrete floor! I dove into my sleeping
22   bag and covered my head. I wondered how I would ever
23   face Mrs. Martin again. I knew she'd never look at me the
24   same! I still blush every time I see her, which thankfully
25   is not that often any more.
26   I learned an important lesson that night! Never ever
27   think that just because you're dared to do something
28   that you *have* to do it! You don't! They don't call it *truth*

1   *or dare* for nothing! Pick *truth!* How bad can that be?
2   'Cause you can always lie. Nobody will ever know. But
3   believe me, take my advice and save yourself now — you
4   streak one time around a basement and *everyone will*
5   *know. Everyone!* And *you* will *never, ever* forget it!

77. Night Terrors
(Girl)

1   JACKIE: You'll never believe this, but I'm sixteen years old
2   and I've never spent the night over at a friend's house.
3   Not once. Ever. And it's not because I haven't been
4   invited, because I have. Time after time after time. So
5   much in fact that I've run out of lame excuses for not
6   going. I've gotten to the point that I actually accept the
7   invitation and then don't show up. I explain later that I
8   got really ill and couldn't go. Or I totally forgot about it,
9   or got grounded at the last minute.

10   I think my friends are starting to think I don't like
11   them or want to spend time with them, but I swear that's
12   not the truth! There's just no way I could ever spend the
13   night away from home. All it would take is once and I'd
14   be labeled a freak for life.

15   See, I have these things called night terrors. They're
16   really horrible and totally unpredictable. I have no idea
17   what sets them off or when they're going to come, but
18   when they do — watch out! I wake up screaming bloody
19   murder and have absolutely no idea why. My parents
20   have gotten used to it, but I know it would scare the
21   bejeepers out of my friends. When I had the very first
22   one, my mom thought I was being murdered in my bed!
23   That's how awful I sound! I scream like a girl! (Which of
24   course I am, but you know what I mean!) I would just die
25   if I had one while I was at a friend's house. I would never
26   live it down!

27   These aren't just nightmares either. They last a lot
28   longer. My parents used to try and wake me to stop me

1   from screaming, but it wouldn't work. If anything, I
2   scream louder if you try to talk to me or shake me. The
3   doctors say it just has to run its course. I can't see my
4   friends letting *that* happen! They'd be terrified and then
5   they'd look at me all weird. I feel like a werewolf. You
6   know, can't go to sleep at night because you never know
7   what I'll turn into. I hate being a screaming maniac!
8   The good thing is I haven't had one in almost three
9   months. They're starting to get fewer and farther in
10 between. Maybe I'll outgrow them all together. I sure
11 hope so. I hate to think what my future husband will do
12 if he wakes up to high-pitched screaming from beside
13 him in the bed! He'd probably take off running and never
14 come back!

78. Navy Brat
(Guy)

1   TODD: Dear Dad, I'm writing this letter because I don't have
2   the guts to tell you on the phone. I knew the words would
3   fly right out of my mouth and I wouldn't make any sense.
4   First off, I want you to know how much I appreciate
5   everything you've always done for me. You've pushed me
6   to be my best and I know that's why I've been able to
7   achieve so much. You're the voice in my head that always
8   tells me to keep going. Never give up.
9   That's what makes this so hard. I know you're going
10   to be disappointed in me and I can hardly stand it. But
11   I'm not quitting, Dad. Not really, because this was never
12   what I wanted. Never my dream. It's always been yours.
13   Yours and Greg's. You both were made for this. I wasn't.
14   I know I should've told you this before. Never should've
15   let things go this far. It wasn't fair to you or me. But here's
16   the deal, Dad. I'm leaving the Navy. Not because boot
17   camp got the better of me, but because I didn't give the
18   best of me to boot camp. I know that will be hard for you
19   to understand. That I don't love everything about being in
20   the Navy. Thing is, I don't even *like* any of it. I'm not cut
21   out to be a service man. I want to be a veterinarian. They
22   don't have much use for one of those around here.
23   They're discharging me on Sunday. Not dishonorably
24   or anything, just a voluntary discharge. After a lot of
25   meetings and a lot of counseling, they accept the fact
26   that this was not a match for me or them. I know to you
27   it will always seem dishonorable and I'm sorry for that. I
28   didn't mean to let you down. I hope that one day you'll

1	be able to forgive me. I know every man in our family has
2	served in the Navy. I guess that's why I felt the pressure
3	in the first place. I knew how much you were counting on
4	me to follow in the family footsteps.
5	Anyway, I'll be flying in Sunday night. I hope you'll be
6	there to pick me up. I'll understand, though, if you don't
7	want to see me. Just know that this was probably the
8	hardest thing I've ever done in my life and I'm sorry to let
9	you down. I love you, Todd.

79. Waiting for Freedom
(Guy)

1   JAMES: I wasn't even there. Maybe if I had been, none of this
2   would be happening. I would've stopped Mom. Or Barby.
3   What gives them the right to just rip us from our home
4   anyway? Over one stupid incident? I know it was bad, but
5   come on, everybody makes a mistake now and then. And
6   Mom is real sorry now. She knows she shouldn't have hit
7   Barby, especially as hard as she did. It's been over a
8   week and Barby's face is still swollen and bruised. She
9   won't even mention Mom's name, she's so upset. I don't
10   blame her really, but sometimes Barby pushes Mom too
11   far. She just keeps on and keeps on. Couldn't she tell
12   that Mom had been drinking? Why didn't she just shut
13   her mouth and go to her room?
14   Now we're stuck in this stupid foster family for God
15   knows how long. I just want to go back home. We've
16   dealt with Mom before, what makes them think we can't
17   do it again? Mom's hit *me* plenty of times and they didn't
18   take us then.
19   What really bugs me is that Mom was going to take me
20   to get my license at the end of this week. My license! My
21   ticket to freedom. Then I could've gotten out of there
22   whenever I wanted. Only now I can't go. This "foster"
23   woman says there's no way she's adding me to *her*
24   insurance, and no insurance means no driving. What a
25   crock! I'm sixteen. Isn't it my *right* to drive? I gotta lose
26   both my home and my freedom all in one week?
27   They say Mom's going to some kind of parenting class
28   and if she finishes it and stops drinking, we can go back

1   home. Well, we might as well wait for cows to fly because

2   Mom isn't ever going to give up the booze. She's been

3   drinking ever since I can remember. Ever since Dad left,

4   I guess. Losing her kids isn't going to stop her.

5   I guess it's all up to me now. Suffer through these next

6   two years, turn eighteen and get my brothers and sister

7   out of here. I'll get a job. And a place for them. It'll be

8   tough, but worth it. We don't need some fake family to

9   love us. We've got each other. When it boils down to it,

10   that's all we've ever had anyway.

80. A Pet What?
(Guy)

1 SAM: I used to think it wasn't real. You know, a memory that
2   was really a dream but as you got older it morphed into
3   this real life event. That's what I thought, because when
4   I remembered it, I knew it was too bizarre to actually be
5   real. Nobody has a pet alligator, right?
6   I remember my dad bringing it home in a shoebox and
7   how he wouldn't tell us what it was at first. We could hear
8   scratching against the sides. I pictured a fluffy kitten and
9   I instantly yelled out, "Puffball," because I wanted to be
10   the one to name it.
11   "Oh, you won't want to call this Puffball," Dad said
12   laughing and he lifted the lid.
13   Two beady little black eyes stared at us. The tail
14   whipped from side to side, making a thudding noise
15   against the box.
16   "You've got to be kidding," my mom shrieked, while we
17   all dove to pick it up.
18   "Careful," Dad warned. "He's small, but he's still got
19   teeth."
20   He did, too. Sharp little spikes that dug into your
21   finger if you got too close to his mouth. He was *so*
22   awesome! We named him Godzilla and fed him bits of
23   hamburger and let him spend most of his time in the tub.
24   For one short week I was the coolest kid on the street.
25   Everybody wanted to come see the pet alligator named
26   Godzilla.
27   I remember setting up a play town with blocks and toy
28   cars and the fire station I got for Christmas. Then I set

1   Godzilla loose on top of it all and pretended he was
2   terrorizing the city! It was so awesome! Every boy's dream.
3   He died just seven days after Dad brought him home.
4   We don't know why. All I knew was my instant popularity
5   ended just as fast. More importantly, though, I missed
6   my beady-eyed little friend. I guess that's why for all
7   these years I convinced myself that it never really
8   happened. Nobody has a pet alligator, right? But deep
9   down I knew Godzilla had not been just a dream because
10   the hurt in my heart was truly real.

81. The Switch-Off
(Guy)

1 DANIEL: There are certainly advantages to being a twin.
2   Especially identical ones like me and my brother.
3   Advantages way greater than just the extra attention
4   you're always sure to get.
5   When we were little the teacher used to put star
6   stickers on our heads so she could tell us apart.
7   Stickers. Hello? Even at five, we knew those suckers
8   could be switched! I think we may have single-handedly
9   caused three teachers to retire early!
10   Most twins have at least a subtle difference — if you
11   look hard enough. Not Dave and me. We are one hundred
12   percent identical. It's amazing. Sometimes we can't even
13   tell ourselves apart! Ha, ha!
14   It's been great since even though we're the same on
15   the outside, we're very different on the inside. See, I'm
16   good at math. Dave's good at science. So when it's time
17   for math ... well, you get the idea! I haven't been to a
18   science class in years!
19   I guess some people think it's weird that we still dress
20   exactly the same even in high school. I can live with that!
21   It's the only way this works. We dress differently and the
22   gig is up!
23   One time I even got a kiss from Dave's girlfriend. To
24   this day she has no idea that I wasn't him! Of course, I
25   can never tell him that, but who knows? He's probably
26   kissed my girl, too!
27   Anyway, we're getting a little nervous about the whole
28   ACT test thing. How am I going to answer a single

1	science question right? And Dave can barely add, much
2	less do algebra or geometry! All these years of switching
3	are finally catching up with us! We'll never make it to
4	college. Never get good jobs. We'll be a couple of
5	identical bums living in the street! Or we'll have to join
6	the circus! Oh, I knew we should've never switched
7	those stars!

82. Mr. Fish
(Guy)

1   FRED: Rocket pops. Push-ups. Freezer pops of all different
2   colors. Ice cream cones with sprinkles and nuts. Frozen
3   bubblegum you have to suck on forever before you can
4   chew it! I love them all! Sometimes I'd just stand there
5   staring at the side of the truck, unable to decide on just
6   one. Mr. Fish would threaten, "I'm leaving. I mean it.
7   Make up your mind, kid." Kid. All those years and he
8   never knew my name.
9   The ice cream truck. What an awesome invention!
10   Wonderful, sweet confections driven straight up your
11   street! You could hear him coming from a mile away. The
12   tune was always the same, blaring out from a speaker
13   mounted on top. Your heart would start racing. Around
14   the house you'd dash, pulling off couch cushions, looking
15   everywhere for a quarter to buy a treat! It didn't matter
16   that you had five different flavors of ice cream in your
17   own freezer. This was the ice cream man. A semi-god
18   who, for a small price, gave you a slice of heaven.
19   There you'd stand, moving from foot to foot on the
20   curb, trying not to look impatient as he stopped just
21   three houses down. *Wait … wait …* you'd tell yourself and
22   then, wham! You were off like a shot! Running as fast as
23   your feet would carry you down to your neighbor's house.
24   Mr. Fish, our ice cream man, was the best. Looking
25   back now that I'm older, I realize he was just a really
26   smart businessman using a stupid marketing ploy to
27   keep us coming back. Day after day.
28   See, Mr. Fish not only gave you ice cream, he gave you

1   a little plastic toy. Zoo animals. Zebras, giraffes, hippos,
2   and — my favorite — the lion. Every day you could pick a
3   different one! They probably only cost him pennies each.
4   If that. To us, they were priceless. Just one more reason
5   why the popsicles in our own freezer could never stack up
6   to Mr. Fish's Frozen Treats.
7   Sometimes even now when no one is home, I run out
8   when I hear the ice cream truck coming down our street.
9   Mr. Fish is long gone and this new guy doesn't pass out
10   plastic zoo toys, but there's something about a drippy,
11   over-priced ice cream cone that still brings a smile to
12   my face.

83. The Con Man
(Guy)

1   JACOB: My father is so tight, he squeaks when he walks!
2   He's like the ultimate con man, always trying to run
3   some kind of deal or something. Do you know how
4   embarrassing that is? We can never just walk up to the
5   counter and pay for something like normal people! Oh
6   no! He either tries to wheel and deal until he gets what
7   he wants or flat out lies his way into getting something
8   without paying! I can't tell you how many times we've
9   gotten a free meal because of a hair my dad plucked from
10   his own head and put in his food! He's even stooped so
11   low as to bring his own bug in his pocket that he can put
12   on his plate! How gross is that?
13   The latest thing is combo offers. He won't just offer
14   money now for things he wants, he offers stuff with it. I'm
15   serious! He bought our neighbor's beat-up old car for
16   eighty dollars and a pair of wrestling tickets! Nobody
17   normal buys things with wrestling tickets! He says he's
18   going to fix the car up and trade it in. What's he going to
19   get? Two pairs of tickets?
20   It's like a huge flea market at our house. We have so
21   much junk. Dad won't throw anything away because he
22   just *knows* one day it will either be worth something or
23   come in handy somehow. Like this — a broken-down
24   toaster! What the heck are we ever going to do with that?
25   Or this bucket — looks useful enough, right? *Wrong!*
26   There's a hole in the bottom! Now you tell me, who will
27   ever need a bucket with a hole in the bottom? *No one!*
28   He's crazy, I tell you. Way past the normal point of

1	being thrifty. Or even cheap. He lives to wheel and deal.
2	I'm just lucky it's illegal to sell or trade your kid or I'd be
3	long gone! Probably would've gotten a broken-down
4	washer and a free jug of detergent ... or if he was *real*
5	lucky, a couple of *front row seats to a basketball game!*

84. Cute as a Button
(Girl)

1   ABIGAIL: My mother is so neurotic! I am sixteen years old
2   and she still won't let me get my belly button pierced!
3   Says she's heard horror stories about infections and stuff
4   that probably aren't even true! Nobody dies from a belly
5   button piercing! Besides, I'd take care of it and do
6   everything they say to. Mine would *not* get infected.
7   They're just so cool looking. All my friends have them.
8   Well, a lot of them anyway. I just don't understand why
9   my mom has to be so overprotective! It's just a stinking
10   little hole. She let me pierce my ears. *Three times!* What's
11   the difference?
12   She says one day I'll regret having it done but I know
13   I won't. I've wanted one forever, so I know I'm not going
14   to change my mind. This is not a phase. Besides, I can
15   always take it out, can't I?
16   It's my body. I should be allowed to pierce it if I want.
17   Who made up that whole eighteen-year-old rule anyway?
18   A bunch of control-freak parents, that's who!
19   Maybe I can just pierce it myself! I know tons of
20   people who pierced their own ears! How hard can it be to
21   do the belly button? I think they use a curved needle ...
22   well, my dad's got plenty of fishhooks!
23   I wonder how bad it would hurt. A fishhook's pretty
24   thick. I'd have to use a lot of ice ... what if it got stuck?
25   I might not be able to get it in all the way ... that wouldn't
26   be a pretty sight.
27   Well, you just wait! The day I turn eighteen, I'm getting
28   it done and my mother will just have to deal with it!

85. Where's the Witch?

(Girl)

1   LILLY: I think there must be something wrong with me
2   because I actually like my stepmother! She's really cool
3   and she treats me like her friend instead of her
4   stepdaughter. She *never* yells at me or tells me to clean
5   my room or get off the phone. In fact, she actually told
6   my dad that he should back off of me a little! How
7   awesome is that?

8   She's nothing like the evil stepmothers you hear about.
9   In fact, some days I like her better than my real mom. Mom
10   never buys me stuff for no reason or lets me go to concerts
11   on school nights or lets me stay out until midnight. I'm
12   telling you, the whole stepmother thing is pretty sweet. I
13   don't know why they get such a bum rap. You know, maybe
14   Cinderella was just a brat! A couple of chores isn't too
15   much to ask for living in a castle, now is it?

16   Anyway, the bad thing is I have to act like I don't like
17   Nancy or my friends will think I'm weird. They all hate their
18   stepmoms or stepdads. That's why I never invite anyone
19   over to my dad's house. They would die if they saw how
20   well we got along. They might even think I'm betraying my
21   mother for being nice to her.

22   I'm not ... am I? I mean, Mom wants me to like Nancy ...
23   right?

24   Sometimes she gets a funny look on her face when I talk
25   about things at Dad's. But that doesn't mean she's jealous
26   or anything. ... She wouldn't want me to be miserable
27   there. ... Though she does look a little hurt sometimes. ...
28   Oh, why did I have to get such a nice stepmother?

86. Do You Believe in Miracles?
(Girl)

1   APRIL: Do you believe in miracles? Real, honest-to-goodness,
2   life-changing miracles? I do. Or least I really want to. You
3   hear about them all the time, so there's got to be some
4   truth to them, right? I mean, they happen to other
5   people, other families, so there's *no* reason why one can't
6   happen to me ... or my mom, really.
7   I'm just so afraid that it won't. So afraid that miracles
8   really do only happen to people in faraway places, to
9   people you only see on the news — not to an ordinary
10   stay-at-home housewife like my mom.
11   But she needs a miracle, God. A big one. And she
12   deserves it, too. She's never done anything to hurt
13   anyone her whole life. She's one of those people who
14   would go hungry so that someone else could eat. And
15   she's always buying stuff for me instead of herself. She
16   wouldn't even buy a wig when her hair fell out because
17   she wanted to buy my prom dress with the money. I
18   didn't want it. Didn't even want to go to the stupid prom.
19   But Mom said it meant so much to her — that she
20   wanted to see me look like a princess in a really beautiful
21   gown because she might never see me get married ...
22   It's just so unfair. She's too young to die. Nobody
23   else's mom is going to be dead before they even
24   graduate! How am I supposed to make it through all this
25   stuff without her? I love my dad, sure, but this is *Mom!* I
26   need her!
27   So you gotta give us this miracle, God. You've got to.
28   Take someone else's mom — wait! I didn't mean that! I

1   don't want someone else to lose their mom ... or dad ...

2   Can't we all just live happily ever after? Is that really

3   so much to ask?

87. A Statue on Stage
(Girl)

1   ROSE: There I was. Frozen in time. I don't even think I blinked.

2   I know my mouth didn't move, just hung open wide like I'd

3   seen a murder or something. The big thing is, no words

4   came out. Complete silence.

5   Then, from the audience — a cough. Offstage — a

6   whisper. I think it was my line. Being whispered to me as

7   if I'd forgotten it!

8   Stupid person. I *knew* the line. Backward and forward.

9   Problem was, I just couldn't get it to come out. The connection

10 from brain to vocal chords had somehow disconnected.

11   All I knew was everyone was staring at me. Even beyond

12 the bright lights glaring in my face, I could see them — feel

13 them ... waiting ... waiting for the statue to speak.

14   I don't know how long I stood there. It felt like time had

15 stopped for good. Finally, someone nudged me, a little

16 roughly, I might add, and as if by magic the words started

17 tumbling out. One line right after the other.

18   The audience sighed. I heard them. This huge breath of

19 relief as if they were as relieved as I was that the frozen ice

20 statue had somehow melted.

21   The rest of the play was flawless. *I* was flawless. Not one

22 missed line or forgotten cue.

23   Looking back at that opening moment, I hope that

24 somehow time became exaggerated in my mind. That

25 what felt like an eternity was only a dramatic entrance or

26 a dramatic pause. That no one else saw the girl who for

27 one brief moment was too scared to even breathe ... much

28 less talk.

88. Spring Break Regrets
(Girl)

1   AMBER: I did something last week that I know is going to
2   haunt me for the rest of my life, pop out of my closet of
3   regrets when I least expect It and totally embarrass my
4   family and me!

5   I don't even know why I did it. It's so unlike me to go
6   along with a crowd. I'm usually the sensible one! Always
7   the designated driver. The one who has never been drunk
8   or ever done drugs. So why all of a sudden did I do
9   something this stupid?

10   I can't even blame it on alcohol because I didn't have
11   the first drink! At least I was smart enough to not do
12   that! I'll have to remind my parents of that little fact
13   when all this comes out! Maybe they'll punish me less for
14   not being completely stupid! Of course, they might prefer
15   to believe that I was drunk rather than completely sober
16   and flashing a whole crowd of people my chest!

17   That's right, folks! I put my twin peaks out there for a
18   whole beach to see! There were shirts flying up everywhere
19   and I was right smack dab in the middle of it! I have no
20   idea why! I don't even change in front of my friends! I've
21   never even been close to being an exhibitionist! So why
22   then? In front of a bunch of strangers?

23   I guess I just got caught up in the whole free feeling
24   moment! Not that I'm making excuses, though! I know
25   better than to do something like that! I don't even wear
26   spaghetti strap tops because I think they make girls look
27   sleazy and now look at me! A future stripper! My parents
28   are going to kill me!

1	They say this kind of stuff just flies around the
2	Internet! How many people are going to see my bare,
3	naked chest? What if someone recognizes me?! Not from
4	*these (Point to chest.)* — but this! *(Point to face.)* This is one
5	memorable face! All it takes is for *one* person to
6	recognize me and it's all over! Take my advice, if you ever
7	get the chance to go to the beach during spring break —
8	keep your shirt on!

89. Addicted to Scrapping
(Girl)

1   ALLIE: I have a serious problem and it's only getting worse and
2   worse. See, I save everything. Movie ticket stubs, pieces of
3   food wrappers, scraps of material, flyers, notes, cards ...
4   anything and everything that might remind me of any
5   special or even not-so-special occasion I've ever had! I have
6   every single birthday card I've ever opened, as well as the
7   envelopes! It's crazy!

8   You'd think my room would be full of boxes of junk. But
9   no! I'm much weirder than that! I actually scrapbook all
10 that stuff into cute little memory books. It's consuming my
11 life trying to capture all these memories! I have to
12 scrapbook almost every night or I get behind! I already
13 have twenty finished scrapbooks and I'm only fifteen years
14 old! That's more than one per year!

15 But here I am, pasting and mounting every shell I've ever
16 found at the beach or the top to a soda can that my then
17 boyfriend bought for me! How nuts is that? I know it's
18 compulsive and obsessive, but I can't stop! It's sucking up
19 my life and my money! I'm flat broke! Do you have any idea
20 how much scrapbooking supplies cost? I had to get a job
21 at the scrapbooking store just so I could get a discount! I
22 have every stamp, cutout, and calligraphy pen available!
23 But what's the sense in saving all this stuff if I can't make
24 it look nice on a page? No one wants to flip through the
25 memories of my life if they're boring!

26 Of course no one's ever going to sit through twenty
27 albums anyway! It's all for naught! I've wasted my life. ...
28 Hey, wait! I know! I'll make a *new* album! A highlights-of-
29 my-life album! I can't wait! It's going to be so much fun!

90. Best Friends
(Guy)

1 GEORGE: This has to be the saddest day of my life. My best
2 friend in the whole world died this morning. It was so
3 unexpected, too. I never even saw it coming. I just thought,
4 I guess, that we'd be together forever. Now he's gone and
5 I don't know how I'm going to make it without him.

6 Bo was the best listener. I told him all my problems, and
7 let me tell you, over the years I've had my share! Who
8 hasn't? But Bo was always there for me. Always by my
9 side. There was a look in his eyes of pure and total trust.
10 He trusted me and I trusted him.

11 There will never be another friend like Bo. Ever. We grew
12 up together. He was the one thing I could count on — no
13 matter what.

14 When my parents got divorced, he was there. When I got
15 in trouble for skipping school, he was there. When my dad
16 remarried and I refused to go to the wedding — who was
17 there with me holed up in my room all day and night? Bo.
18 You just don't find friends like that. A friend who accepts
19 you as you are. Never turns their back on you.

20 Loyal. That was Bo. No one would ever dare touch me
21 with Bo around. He would've ripped them to shreds. Nope,
22 no one would hurt me with Bo standing by.

23 I'm going to miss him so much. I can't believe he's gone.
24 The house will feel so empty now.

25 Bo, you were and always will be my best friend. You truly
26 were the best dog a guy could ever have.

27 Thanks, boy, for being there. I'll miss you, buddy.

91. Hit and Run
(Guy)

1   LANCE: It was really dark. And rainy. I could barely see out
2   of the window and my windshield wipers were on high.
3   They just couldn't clear the rain off fast enough. Back
4   and forth. Back and forth.
5   I guess the smart thing would've been to pull over for a
6   minute until the storm passed, but my mom had always
7   told me that it was just as dangerous to be sitting on the
8   side of the road. I didn't want someone plowing into me! I
9   knew if I couldn't see, well, no one else could either!
10   Anyway, I guess that's why I kept going. I just wanted
11   to get home. I was so stressed from the rain. My hands
12   were clenched on the wheel. Even my knuckles were
13   white! And I wasn't going fast! I swear! What kind of
14   moron would be driving fast on a night like that? The
15   conditions were terrible. I don't know why they're saying
16   I was driving too fast. I wasn't. I know I wasn't because
17   I remember thinking it was going to take me forever to
18   get home and I knew that Mom was going to be worried.
19   But I didn't hurry! I didn't! If I was an old person, they'd
20   believe me! It's because I'm a teenager that they think I
21   was driving recklessly! But I wasn't. It was storming like
22   crazy! How can they blame me for not being able to see?
23   Now they're charging me with manslaughter!
24   Manslaughter for hitting a person that I couldn't even
25   see! And didn't expect to see! What kind of person is out
26   on a night like that? And she came out of nowhere! One
27   minute there was nothing and the next minute there was
28   a body flying over the hood of my car. It all happened so

1   fast. I didn't even stop at first because my mind just
2   couldn't believe what I'd seen. I thought maybe it had
3   really been a deer or something — not a person! Like I
4   said, who'd be outside on a night like that? The lightning
5   was crashing everywhere! I was scared to be in the car,
6   much less outside! So I told myself it was an animal. Not
7   a person. I was going to go back and see, though. I was.
8   But they're making it sound like I just left her there.
9   Left her in the middle of the road to be hit again. Well, first
10   off, I didn't know it was a *her!* I thought it was an *it!* And
11   I didn't leave her there. I was going to go back, I was just
12   looking for a safe place to turn the car around. The road
13   was narrow and there weren't a lot of options! The rain
14   was still coming down so hard, I couldn't see anything!
15   I didn't see those driveways they're saying I passed up. I
16   didn't. Not one of them. Why won't anyone believe me?
17   Why would I lie about that?
18   So it was taking a little while. Can I help it that
19   someone else came upon her first? I wasn't leaving her
20   there. They're making me sound like a monster! I'm not!
21   I was just a scared kid who wanted to get home. But I
22   wasn't going home ... I was going back ... I swear ...

92. Your Other Left
(Guy)

1   EARL: They say that the police officer who rides with you for the
2   driver's test flunks almost everybody their first time.
3   Especially guys. It's like a power trip for him to put a big fat
4   F on your form. Now that I've seen him, I believe it. I don't
5   think his face has cracked a smile for years! And his voice is
6   so gruff you can barely understand him. He told me to turn
7   the wipers on and I couldn't understand him so I turned the
8   blinker on! He thought I was just that stupid! Like I don't
9   know this car inside and out! My dad bought it for me when
10   I was fifteen. We've been taking it apart and putting it back
11   together for almost two years. I think I know where the
12   stupid windshield wiper switch is!
13   Then Mr. Fail Everybody climbs into the car and tells me
14   to head out of the parking lot and turn left. What did I do?
15   Turned right, of course! Like a moron! You'd think that would
16   justify an instant failing grade right there but no, he says, "I
17   meant your other left," and tells me to keep going. I guess I
18   should be grateful for that. It would have been embarrassing
19   to turn right around and go back to the parking lot. By the
20   time we reached the end of the street my hands were
21   shaking so badly I could barely keep them still on the wheel.
22   The rest of the drive went pretty well. I didn't even mess
23   up the parallel parking. Got real close to the curb without
24   hitting it. Still, I know he's going to fail me. I can tell by all
25   that writing he's doing now. He may even take my permit
26   back! Can he do that? What a jerk! What a moron! Everyone
27   was right — he's a pathetic cop who can't … wait! He's
28   handing me my test …
29   I passed? Really? Oh, I love this guy!

93. Makeup Free
(Girl)

1　JACKIE: My friends think I'm weird because I don't wear
2　makeup. They're always trying to get me to put some of
3　their face gunk on. It's like they think I can't be a "real"
4　girl unless I wear all that stuff on my face. I'm not anti-
5　makeup. If they like it, fine. For them. Why does it have
6　to be for me?

7　　I just don't see the need. Seems like a lot of work for
8　nothing. For one, it's not fooling anyone. You're either
9　pretty or you're not. Period. And so what if people might
10　think I'm pretty if I wear it? I don't care what others think
11　about me. Never have. Isn't that better than hiding
12　behind a bunch of beauty products?

13　　I guess you could say I actually like the skin I'm in. It's
14　not perfect. Not by a long shot. I've got freckles and
15　sometimes a few zits. Who doesn't? Why do I have to
16　hide them under a pile of concealer? Get a clue, girls, it
17　doesn't *really* conceal them! If anything, it draws more
18　attention to the area!

19　　Why can't we all just accept the fact that we're not
20　perfect — never gonna be perfect — and go on about our
21　lives. Wouldn't that be better for everyone? Surely there
22　are better things to spend my money and my time on!
23　Geesh, it takes long enough just to keep up with
24　everyday hygiene — teeth brushing, hair washing,
25　shaving — who wants to add more?

26　　Maybe I can start the no makeup revolution! Show
27　others how freeing it can be! Make a stand for clear faces
28　everywhere! Free the makeup! Free the makeup! Well, all

1 except for this one little thing of lip gloss ... or this one ...
2 I couldn't live without my lip gloss! But it's *not* makeup!
3 It's ... protection! See? SPF twenty-five! This, my friends,
4 is a necessity!

94. The Birds and the Bees
(Girl)

1 HILLARY: You are never going to believe this! If I hadn't been
2 the one sitting there, I wouldn't believe it either! I always
3 thought it was one big joke. Nobody really uses "the
4 birds and the bees" to talk about sex!
5 Well, guess what? They do! My mom actually used that
6 line of bull with me last night when we had our big "sex
7 talk." I almost died. Literally. I mean, how do you keep a
8 straight face during that? Bees, Mom, really? And the
9 whole flower and pollen thing? Did she really think that
10 made sense? I half-expected her to start drawing
11 pictures, and I'm not talking about the kind that might
12 make a teenage girl blush, but cute little black and
13 yellow bee pictures!
14 My mother needs to get a clue. Number one, hello! I've
15 had sex ed three times already and they actually use the
16 right names for body parts, and number two, I'm a junior
17 in high school! I've heard more about sex just by sitting
18 on the bus than my mother uttered in her whole forty-five
19 minute speech! I don't think she ever really said one R-
20 rated word. Does she think I'm five years old?
21 I guess it could've been worse! I have a friend whose
22 mom actually had a book with pictures and she gave her
23 a mini quiz when they were done talking! Now, how do
24 you win in that situation? If you fail the test, she thinks
25 you didn't listen. If you pass, you look like you know too
26 much and your mom might be suspicious and think
27 you've been up to something!
28 I really don't understand why Mom felt the need in the

1	first place. I don't even have a boyfriend! And I've already
2	told her that I'm going to wait until I get married. She
3	saw me sign the pledge card at church. Doesn't she trust
4	me? Besides, I hate to tell her, but her little birds and the
5	bees speech, although highly entertaining, was
6	completely uninformative! When it comes time for me, I
7	may just have to check out a book from the library! It
8	makes me wonder if my mom has actually *had* sex! Hey,
9	maybe I'm adopted!

95. Broken-Handed
(Guy)

1	BRETT: It wasn't my shining moment of glory, that's for
2	sure! In fact, I'm hoping I can chalk it up to the stupidest
3	thing I'll ever do in life. But somehow, I doubt it. I'm not
4	the sharpest knife in the drawer, according to my dad,
5	and unfortunately I'm pretty emotional. Those two things
6	generally do not bode well for common sense! Even still,
7	it was stupid. Obviously, hitting a metal locker was *not*
8	going to get me my girlfriend back!
9	She broke up with me after third hour. Right there in
10	the hallway like some kind of casual encounter. Forget
11	the fact that we've been going out for over a year, but *in*
12	*the hall?* Did I not deserve *any* privacy? Did she have to
13	humiliate me in front of everyone? How could she just
14	dump me and then walk away?
15	I did the first thing I thought of. It just felt natural. I
16	dented it, too. My locker. They're probably going to make
17	me pay for it. Put in a brand new shiny locker — like a
18	monument to the whole stinking event.
19	It's bad enough I have to walk around with this stupid
20	cast on. Do you know how embarrassing that is? Breaking
21	your hand over your girlfriend? I thought maybe Megan
22	would be a little sympathetic. Realize how much I cared
23	and that she'd made a big mistake. But you know what?
24	She says she's scared of me now! Says she didn't realize
25	I had a "violent" side! Doesn't she get it? I hit a locker! *Not*
26	*her!* I wasn't even wishing it was her ... I swear!
27	I was just upset. I had all this anger raging inside me
28	and it just came out — wham! I hit it hard, too. Hard

1	enough to break three bones in my hand. Of course, my
2	parents aren't too happy about that. Mom says she ought
3	to make me pay the doctor's bills. Well, I say if anybody
4	should pay, it should be Megan. What kind of person
5	breaks up like that? Did I mean *nothing* to her? She might
6	as well have put it in a "Dear John" letter. Girls say they
7	want a guy who's emotional, but they don't! You have one
8	uncontrollable outburst and everyone thinks you're
9	psycho! I swear it makes me just want to *kick* something!

96. Homeless
(Guy)

1   SHAWN: I live in a box. I'm not talking metaphorically or
2   poetically. I literally live in a box. A cardboard box that
3   used to have someone's refrigerator in it.
4   You don't believe me. I can see it in your face. You're
5   thinking, "Yeah, right. The boy uses three syllable words.
6   He does not live in a box."
7   But I do. I have for almost a year now. I haven't been
8   to school once in twelve months. Basically, I'm a truant.
9   More importantly, I'm starving. I can't remember the last
10   true meal I've had. Actually, that's a lie. I know exactly
11   what and when and where it was, and I think about it a
12   lot. The smells. The tastes. It was the night before our
13   house burned down.
14   Mom had made roast and mashed potatoes. And the
15   peas with the little onions that burst open when you chew
16   them. The rolls were hot and I ate at least three of them.
17   With lots of butter. It was a good meal. I could tell Mom
18   was really trying because up until then we'd probably had
19   macaroni and cheese for three or four nights in a row.
20   Mostly because we were broke, but also because Mom
21   wasn't getting out of bed too much back then.
22   See, my dad took off and left us. No note. Nothing.
23   Not even a phone call. We had no idea where he was. If
24   he'd left his clothes we would've thought something bad
25   had happened. But his stuff was gone, which pretty
26   much meant he'd left on purpose.
27   Bills were piling up. I guess that's why the house
28   insurance hadn't been paid. Mom had retreated to her

1   room and barely came out. But not that night. That night

2   had been different. I should've known it wouldn't last.

3   But I had no idea how bad it was going to get.

4   We lost everything. With no family and no real friends

5   to turn to, we hit the streets. We've been on them ever

6   since. Living out of garbage cans, surviving off other

7   people's trash. It's a disgusting way of life. There's no

8   way I could go to school. I have one outfit to my name

9   and it hasn't been washed in a long, long time. Unless

10   you count standing out in a downpour letting the rain

11   soak you through and through. I don't.

12   So maybe now you're believing me. Thinking that maybe

13   this kid is telling the truth. But what about the words? The

14   impressive words that seem to flow from my mouth?

15   It's simple really. There's not much to do in a

16   cardboard box. Not much at all. And people don't tend to

17   throw out best-selling novels. For some reason, though,

18   they do throw out dictionaries. I've got three. And believe

19   it or not, I've been reading through them every day. I'm

20   up to letter *I*. *Ironic*, isn't it? That a kid in a cardboard

21   box can be *intelligent*. Problem is, most people would

22   rather I just be *invisible*.

97. Hooked on Fishing
(Guy)

1   NOAH: I never liked hooking my own worm. I know that
2   makes me sound girlish, but I don't care. They're
3   squishy and gross! And you're putting a hook through a
4   live squirming body! That squirts out icky stuff! Yuck!
5   Good thing is my grandfather never minded putting my
6   worms on for me. Even when I lost them right away. I'd
7   no more get the line in the water and the worm would
8   come off. My grandfather spent more time baiting my
9   hook than he did fishing himself.
10   We had a lot of good times out on the lake. Didn't
11   always catch a lot of fish, but I think it was partly
12   because I'm not that good a fisherman and partly
13   because my grandfather talked. A lot. It was his time to
14   tell me stories. Lots and lots of stories about my family.
15   Now that I'm older I wonder how much of them were
16   true. They were pretty far-fetched. Like the one about my
17   grandmother throwing dishes out the window because
18   she was mad at him. I never could picture her doing that.
19   She was always so calm. But he insisted she was a real
20   wildcat in her younger days.
21   There was also the time when he says my dad caught
22   a snapping turtle and took out the heart and the heart
23   kept beating until sunset. Then it just stopped. Right
24   when the sun went down. Stuff like that doesn't happen,
25   does it?
26   Grandpa was full of it. He loved life, that's for sure. His
27   laugh could be heard all over the lake, which is why the
28   fish were as far from us as a bird is from a cat. No

1   wonder we almost always went home empty handed.
2   Still, those times with my grandfather were the best I
3   can remember. Getting farmers' tans on our necks and
4   arms. Eating lunch out of a paper sack with an ice-cold
5   soda from the cooler we kept wedged under the seat.
6   Grandma always packed the best lunches. It's hard to
7   believe those days are gone forever now.
8   One day I'll take my son, if I have a son, out on the
9   lake and tell him Grandpa's stories. Maybe he'll believe
10   me. Maybe he won't. Half the fun is wondering. There's
11   just one thing I know for sure, my boy better know how
12   to bait a hook or we'll be up the creek without a paddle!

98. Embarrassed to Smile
(Girl)

1 CHELSEA: "Grandma, what big *teeth* you've got!" Do you
2 know how many times I've heard that stupid line? About
3 a gazillion and one times, and I'm not even exaggerating!
4 My teeth take up about half my face! My lips won't even
5 cover them all. I always have this half-open expression
6 because I can't close my mouth all the way! How sad is
7 that? My teeth are too big for my mouth!
8 I was posing for senior pictures and the photographer
9 said, "Let's try this one with your mouth closed." Well,
10 wouldn't I like to! Do you know how embarrassing that
11 is? That I can't even make my lips meet? I've got the
12 teeth of a giant on a normal-sized head. I can't smile. I
13 can't *not* smile. I just hide behind stuff a lot. My hand.
14 A book. Whatever works. I've even tried filing them
15 down, but guess what? Teeth have nerves in them and
16 they don't take to filing very well! Talk about pain! And I
17 didn't even make a dent. They're just as big as ever,
18 only now they're real sensitive to cold foods.
19 I'm not talking normal buckteeth either. It's way worse
20 than that. I'd be happy to have buckteeth, that's how bad
21 it is. Buckteeth would be a blessing! Oh no. I've got
22 mammoth tusks growing in there with a combo Dracula
23 thing going. I could probably chew a steak in five second
24 flat. Whatever vitamin causes teeth to grow, my mother
25 must've had triple doses when she was pregnant with me!
26 You might be thinking there are worse things. Well, is
27 there? Is there really? Big butt? I can live with. Exercise.
28 Sit on it. Big feet? Who even notices? Big ears? Wear

1   your hair down. But big teeth? Nowhere to hide! They're

2   out there for everyone to see!

3   I can sympathize with the wolf. Think of all the

4   harassment over his big teeth. It wasn't his fault. No

5   wonder he tried to chew up Little Red Riding Hood.

6   Maybe everyone should think about that before they open

7   their stupid little mouths with little bitty teeth! Just

8   watch out or I might sink my teeth into you!

99. The Magical Note
(Guy)

1   CAMERON: Some school rules are absolutely ludicrous!
2   They're trying to suspend me because I've missed too
3   many days without a doctor's excuse. Does that make
4   sense? They think I've missed too much so they're forcing
5   me to miss three more days? Are there morons in the
6   front office just dreaming this stuff up? I can't help it if
7   I've been sick a lot this year. I've always been sickly.

8   I guess that's why Mom doesn't run me to the doctor
9   now every time I *do* get sick. I've got a regular medicine
10   cabinet at home of leftover prescriptions. I just take one
11   of those, get better, and go back to school. Can I help it
12   that my mother doesn't see the need to pay a doctor just
13   so the school can have a stupid piece of paper that says
14   I was sick?

15   No wonder you have to wait so long when you *do* go to
16   the doctor's. Everybody takes their kid just so they can
17   get the precious note for school. Kid has a cough — off
18   to doctor. Kid has a runny nose — off to the doctor.
19   Hasn't anyone ever heard of a thing called a cold? No
20   doctor's visit required. Just good ol' hot soup and a box
21   of tissues! Not everything has to be a "doctor approved"
22   sickness. You wake up with a fever — you're sick. Don't
23   they want us to stay home and stop the spread of
24   germs? Apparently not!

25   I'm being punished for being sick. It's completely unfair.
26   What was I supposed to do, bring the thermometer in as
27   proof? Oh, no. I forgot. I need the magical *note* to prove I
28   was sick. The school must be getting a cut, some sort of

1   payoff from these doctors! Why else are they pushing every
2   kid with a sniffle to see the doctor? There's got to be
3   something in it for them! A kickback! Maybe that's how we
4   got all those new computers last year. Anonymous donor,
5   my foot!

6   Someone needs to investigate this! I smell a scandal
7   going on here! They can't force me to go to the doctor
8   just so they can get new computers! It's an outrage! I
9   can be sick without a note! I can! Just watch me!

100. Marriage?
(Girl)

1   JANET: My boyfriend is one hundred percent insane!
2   Certifiable! Last night, he asked me to marry him! He
3   had a ring and everything! Is he nuts? We're only
4   seventeen! Hardly old enough to make a decision like
5   that! Now he's saying that if I don't want to marry him
6   that I must not love him. I don't think that just because
7   I actually have a brain that that means I don't love him!
8   I'm not saying that he's stupid or anything — in fact,
9   he's really very sweet. But marriage? What was he
10 thinking? The only couples that get married this young
11 are the ones that *have* to! What would everyone think?
12 They'd be watching my belly like a hawk, just waiting to
13 prove that I'm pregnant! Which I'm not!

14   He says he's afraid that once I go off to college, I'll
15 forget about him. It's like he wants to brand me or
16 something! The way I see it, he doesn't trust me. I'm not
17 buying that whole I-can't-live-without-you thing! We're
18 only going to college thirty miles apart. If we can't make
19 it through that, we certainly don't need to be married!

20   I'll admit that for one brief second the little girl inside
21 of me — the one who's been dreaming of getting married
22 all her life — wanted to scream, yes, yes, yes! I've been
23 sneaking *Bride* magazines since I started high school.
24 What girl doesn't drool over the beautiful gowns and plan
25 every detail years before they need to? I know the kind of
26 dress, bridesmaids' dresses, flowers, napkins ... all that
27 great stuff! But now? What could we possibly afford now?
28 Not much, and I can tell you one thing, my parents will

1   *not* pay for their seventeen-year-old daughter to get
2   married! Where would we have the reception? The
3   cafeteria at school? See how crazy it is?!
4   I just have to tell him no. I tried to last night but he
5   wouldn't listen. He kept saying, "Just think about it."
6   Like I could think about anything else. I couldn't even
7   sleep last night. I don't want to lose Harley. We've been
8   dating for two years. But I'm not ready for marriage.
9   But what if we're supposed to be together? What if I
10   wait and then it's too late ... we meet someone else at
11   college and marry the wrong person! Or worse! What if I
12   end up saying no now and no one else ever asks me! I'll
13   end up single for the rest of my life living in a house full
14   of cats and watching soap operas dreaming of a chance
15   at love! My life will be ruined!
16   I've just got to say yes! It's my one chance at love!
17   Wait! What was I thinking? Whew. For a moment there,
18   I saw my whole life flash before my eyes! But I'm not
19   buying that bull! I've got *my whole life* in front of me!
20   And you know what? It looks great! I'm only seventeen! I
21   am *not* getting married!

About the Author

100 Great Monologs is a perfect fit for Rebecca North Young since she directs drama for her church. Over the past few years, she has written and directed numerous plays for middle and high school students.

Rebecca currently works as a substitute teacher for elementary and middle school students in Georgetown, Kentucky. She has a BA in communications/marketing from the University of Kentucky.

Rebecca moved from upstate New York when she was eleven years old and has called Kentucky home ever since. She lives with her husband (Frank), three daughters (Heather, Kristina, and Ashley) and two cats (who have names but are more often than not called Orange Kitty and Gray Kitty).